EGGS FOR BREAKFAST: Delicious, Healthy Recipes to Jump-Start Your Day

A Chef's Guide to Cooking Eggs with Over 50 Easy-to-Follow Recipes

By Donna Leahy
Photography by Robert Leahy

Eggs for Breakfast: Delicious, Healthy Recipes to Jump-Start Your Day
A Chef's Guide to Cooking Eggs with Over 50 Easy-to-Follow Recipes

By Donna Leahy

Photography by Robert Leahy

Food Arts Fusion LLC

ISBN - 978-1-942118-06-0

© 2015, Donna Leahy

ALL RIGHTS RESERVED. Any unauthorized reprint or use of this material is prohibited. No part of this book may be reproduced or transmitted in any form or by any means, electronic or mechanical, including photocopying, recording or by any information storage and retrieval system without the written permission of the author, except where permitted by law.

Disclaimer

The information contained in this book is based on research and personal experience unless otherwise stated. It should not be substituted for qualified medical advice. Health-related information provided in this book is for educational and entertainment purposes only. Always seek the counsel of a qualified medical practitioner for an individual consultation before making any significant changes to your diet and lifestyle and to answer questions about specific medical conditions. The author and publisher disclaim responsibility for any adverse effects that may result from the use or application of the recipes and information within this book. The publisher and the author make no representations or warranties with respect to the accuracy or completeness of the contents of this work and specifically disclaim all warranties including, without limitation, warranties of fitness or health for a particular purpose. This is work is sold with the understanding that the publisher and author are not engaged in rendering medical or other professional advice, and that neither is liable for damages arising from it.

Thank you for purchasing this book. I am pleased to have you along for the journey to better health and better eating. I know you could have picked from dozens of cookbooks, so to show my appreciation I'd like to offer you a bonus: *Eggs for Breakfast: Ten Quick and Delicious Recipes for Weekdays*. Simply sign up on my website www.donnaleahy.com and I will send you the PDF. I will include you on my list for free stuff and also periodically send you exclusive special offerings as well.

As an experienced chef and author, I write cookbooks on a variety of topics and themes, so my other cookbooks may interest you as well. Please feel free to let me know what aspects of the book you enjoyed and what things you wish I had included. If you have any suggestions for future topics, I'd love to hear them as well.

Finally, if you have a moment to [review this book on Amazon](#), I'd really appreciate it. This type of feedback will help me continue to write the kind of cookbooks that you want to use. Thanks again, I look forward to hearing from you.

Chef Donna

Table of Contents

INTRODUCTION 13
    ABOUT INGREDIENTS 19
    ABOUT THE RECIPES.. 23

CHAPTER ONE
EGG BASICS... 25

THE ANATOMY OF AN EGG 25
DECODING EGG LABELS 29
HOW TO STORE EGGS 33
HOW TO PREPARE EGGS.. 35
    Soft-Cooked Eggs 35
    Hard-Cooked Eggs 37
    Poached Eggs 38
    Scrambled Eggs 40
    Coddled Eggs 42
    Baked Eggs 44
    Fried Eggs 45

CHAPTER TWO
THE CLASSICS 49

Eggs Benedict... 51
Croque Madame... 53
Eggs Poached in Tomato Sauce 57
Eggs in a Basket 59
Huevos Rancheros 61
French Omelet... 63

Eggs in Potato Nests with Bacon 67

Italian Frittata 69

Spanish Tortilla 71

CHAPTER THREE
SIMPLY EGGS 73

Eggs with Roasted Cherry Tomatoes and Blue Cheese 75

Cheese and Egg Soufflé 77

Macaroni and Cheese with Eggs 79

Quinoa with Tomato, Basil, Mozzarella and Eggs 83

Wilted Spinach and Gorgonzola Omelet Roll 85

Baked Tomato, Egg and Mozzarella in Phyllo Cups 87

Potato Skins with Egg, Tomato and Brie 91

Portobello Mushrooms with Basil Egg Topping 93

Soft-Cooked Eggs with Chili-Infused Honey 95

Mushroom Risotto with Eggs 97

Eggs with Pesto, Leeks and Asparagus 99

Eggs and Mushrooms in Brioche 103

Asparagus and Sweet Onion Tart 105

Egg Custard with Morels 106

Eggs with Brioche and Caramelized Onions 108

CHAPTER FOUR
EGGS WITH MEAT 109

Baked Polenta with Eggs, Sausage and Fontina 111

Corned Beef Brisket Hash with Poached Eggs
and Horseradish 115

Thai Fried Rice with Eggs, Pork Belly and Frizzled Leeks 117

Steak, Eggs and Waffles with Chimichurri 119

Spring Rolls with Eggs, Mushrooms and Sausage 123

Duck Confit Hash with Eggs and Mushrooms 125

Corn Pudding with Cilantro and Chorizo 127

Eggs with Prosciutto, Sun-Dried Tomatoes & Chevre 131

Salami and Egg Tarts in Polenta Crust 133

Gorgonzola Sausage Frittata 135

Eggs with Kale and Pancetta 139

Andouille Sausage Strata 141

Breakfast Burritos with Chicken, Eggs and Salsa 143

Breakfast Quesadillas 147

Lentils with Prosciutto and Eggs 149

Rolled Basil Soufflé with Roasted Red Pepper Coulis 153

Ham and Brie Soufflé Roll 155

Prosciutto and Ricotta Cheese Pie 157

Steak and Eggs with Cheese Grits 159

Bacon Jam, Avocado and Egg Muffin Sandwiches 161

Scrapple and Egg Hoagie 163

CHAPTER FIVE
EGGS WITH SEAFOOD 165

Smoked Salmon and Goat Cheese Soufflés 167

Eggs with Salmon in Dill Crepes 169

Smoked Salmon and Eggs with Spinach 173

Mediterranean Eggs 175

Custard Eggs in Potatoes with Caviar 179

Crab and Eggs in Chive Crepes 183

Smoked Trout Frittata with Potatoes, Horseradish & Chives ... 185

Almond-Crusted Crab Cakes with Eggs 187

Egg Pie with Roasted Garlic, Tomatoes and Eggplant 188

Oven-Puffed Lobster and Brie Custards 191

Lobster and Thyme Quiche 193
Eggs Lobster Oscar with Tarragon Rounds 197
Nested Eggs with Potato Blini and Dill Cream 199

CHAPTER SIX
PANTRY 203

English Muffins 205
Flour Tortillas 207
Hoagie Rolls 208
Brioche 211
Puff Pastry 213
Rustic Sandwich Bread 215
Scrapple 216
Sausage 218
    Andouille Sausage 218
    Chorizo 219
    Italian Sausage 220
    Pesto 221
    Tomato Salsa 222
    Hollandaise Sauce 223
    Crème Fraiche 224
    Bacon Jam 225

INDEX 227

INTRODUCTION

Welcome to *Eggs for Breakfast,* the first in a series of cookbooks highlighting delicious, healthy recipes for the most important meal of the day. We're about to go on a culinary journey that will give you a reason to jump out of bed every morning, beginning with practical techniques and delicious, step by step recipes focusing on eggs. While many have explored the versatility of the egg in dishes ranging from a savory soufflé to pastry cream, for me the hen's egg shines most brightly when the sun is peaking over the horizon. Morning is the time when eggs can mean the most for us, both as a healthy meal and a culinary adventure. At its simplest, the egg is an easy-to-prepare, healthy alternative to consuming processed breakfast food. In its most magnificent form, the egg is a blank canvas for our creative culinary brushes to paint. While eggs play an important role in a variety of dishes, the egg reigns supreme at the first meal of the day.

If you want to consume a healthy yet tasty breakfast, the humble egg may be the most perfect, natural source for providing it. And with minimal effort, the egg can become something less humble, a blank palette for culinary creativity that knows no bounds. Simple to prepare, yet able to exceed our expectations—it seems we've been looking at the perfect breakfast food all this time and perhaps never really appreciated its greatness.

I can hear some of your objections rising, so let's resolve this once and for all—YES, you do have time to make breakfast! If you don't believe it, I am about to show you how. As a chef and cookbook author, my goal is to provide a path to healthier eating by encouraging you to prepare your own food. But forgoing processed food does not mean you need to spend all day in the kitchen. In the time it takes you to head to your pantry and un-wrap a processed health food bar, you could have scrambled some eggs. Need a breakfast on the go? Hard cook a few eggs while you're making dinner the night before. Have some extra time on a weekend morning? A little extra effort spent will wow your friends and family with dishes that taste so good they will change the way they look at eggs forever. The egg, a spectacular combination of taste, nutrition and affordability, can single-handedly change the way you view breakfast.

Eggs are affordable because hens produce a lot of eggs—up to 270 per year. The average cost of an egg as of this writing is about 20 cents. Yes, 20 cents! (Anyone remember when a chocolate bar cost 20 cents?) Nutritious eggs contain the highest biological value for protein—that's right, more than that fat juicy steak some health and fitness experts think you should consume often to up your protein. Don't get me wrong—I enjoy a good steak. But it's impossible to beat the value an egg brings to the table.

One egg has only 75 calories, but 6 grams of high-quality protein. It contains 5 grams of fat, of which 1.6 grams are saturated fat. "What about cholesterol?" you may be asking. Because of its high dietary cholesterol content, the egg was once deemed a health risk, giving rise to yet another processed food—the world of egg substitutes. Scientists have since learned that cholesterol in food has a minimal effect on blood cholesterol. In fact, saturated fat (yes, the kind found in that big, juicy steak) has a much bigger effect on blood cholesterol. However, many people today still mistakenly believe eggs cause high cholesterol because the message was so pervasive (it's ironic that the fact that the "experts" were wrong is less widely known). Loaded with iron, vitamins, minerals, carotenoids and disease-fighting nutrients like lutein and the antioxidant zeaxanthin, the discovery of the health benefits of consuming eggs continues to rise. Recent studies found that eggs may reduce the risk of age-related macular degeneration, the leading cause of blindness in older adults. Additionally, brain development and memory may be enhanced by the choline content of eggs.

In terms of taste, eggs have a versatility that makes them a great choice for breakfast. But in the culinary world, breakfast often suffers the same underdog status that eggs have until recently enjoyed. As a professional chef, I've never understood why breakfast doesn't command the attention of other meals. Perhaps it's simply that most high-end restaurants don't open their doors for breakfast. Of course, that doesn't mean that they don't borrow from breakfast fare. You'll find eggs on the menu at the finest Michelin-starred restaurants and the most humble neighborhood bistros. In restaurants around the world, slow-cooked eggs make their appearance atop soups while deep fried eggs garnish an elegant stir-fry of exotic mushrooms. Those qualities that make eggs a component of some of the most memorable dinner dishes around the world are the same ones that make them shining stars on the breakfast table.

Because I ran both a fine dining restaurant and a country inn, breakfast always had a special meaning for me. During dinner service, I literally could not leave the kitchen (well, I could, but then no food would be prepared!). So the relationship I had with our guests mostly occurred in the morning hours. Breakfast was when I met the people who consumed my food, when the relationship between what they ate and who prepared it came together. Much the way we all feel when feeding our friends and family, breakfast represented the nurturing part of my relationship with our guests. It's when everything about the food I prepared became personal. In that sense, it truly was the most important meal of the day.

It's that personal connection that makes cooking for others such a rewarding experience, for a professional chef as well as a home chef. I did not begin my culinary journey as a professional. From the time I was young, I loved cooking for other people. When I decided to open a restaurant, my husband was quick to point out that my experience as a video producer wasn't exactly a substitute for culinary school. But without the time or finances to head off to school, I embraced the

old adage "those that can, do." I went to work, studying and honing my craft.

While breakfast was a chance for me to put all of my creative energy into a singular culinary experience, eggs were most often the star ingredient in these menus. No other single food has so much to offer us for the first meal of the day. Eggs prepared even in the simplest form can delight and amaze the palate of the most discerning foodie. With a little effort, they can be elevated to the highest level of culinary craft.

In our culinary tour of eggs, we will begin with techniques to prepare the most simple preparations of eggs—scrambling, frying, poaching and more. These techniques will then be used to prepare classic dishes like eggs Benedict and omelets. Finally, new ideas on how to prepare eggs to suit a variety of tastes will be featured, both as recipes and in photographs of the completed dishes. These dishes will present the egg in all of its glory, from the epitome of simplicity to the very definition of elegance. From its humble beginnings in the hen house, the egg will rise to become the star ingredient on your breakfast table as well.

ABOUT INGREDIENTS

Long before the farm-to-table movement became official, as a chef I was committed to sourcing our food locally and creating every single dish that appeared in our dining room. The quality of these ingredients was a big key to our success. Our inn's location in Lancaster was home to a large Amish and Mennonite community—farmers who see themselves as stewards of the land and, as such, are responsible for its preservation. Our neighbors were farmers who personally tilled their land, milked their cows, picked vegetables and fruit and collected eggs from the hen house. Our eggs were delivered each morning still warm from the hens that laid them.

Quality ingredients are the basis for any great meal and are especially important at breakfast. While you may not be as fortunate as we were to live in an area surrounded by farms, here are some simple steps to ensure you are using quality whole food. Whenever possible: 1. Buy local. 2. Buy fresh and seasonal. 3. Grow your own. 4. Choose free-range, grass-fed and wild caught.

When you purchase locally, you can personally see how the products are being grown. They also tend to taste better. Many types of heirloom produce (tomatoes are the main one that comes to mind) are not suited to being shipped across continents. But you will often find these tastier selections at your local farmers market. Another option is to participate in Community Supported Agriculture (CSA). Basically, you make an agreement with local farmers to support their production in exchange for a share of it. Typically there are drop-off points set up to accommodate urban dwellers, and some even offer home delivery. If you decide to go this route, it's always worthwhile to visit the farm locations personally and see if the range of products suits your needs.

Seasonal produce will always vary by location. From living in various parts of our country, I've learned that the four-season approach espoused in many cookbooks is not a one-size-fits-all solution. Wild blueberries, which begin ripening in early August, were our favorite seasonal fruit to serve at our B&B in Maine. Because our PA inn was located in the Mid-Atlantic region, our East Coast-centric idea of seasonal meant asparagus in April, carrots in May, strawberries in June and so on. When pumpkins appeared at the farm stands in late September, we knew our local options were coming to an end. When we moved to Whidbey Island in the Puget Sound, all of that was compressed into a shorter growing season because of the northern location. Leafy greens like kale and root vegetables like beets flourished in the cooler, damp climate. Now that we live in a tropical zone, we've had to adjust to an even more challenging definition. What's considered typical summer produce like tomatoes and corn appears in January and February at our local farm markets. So rather than organize the recipes by seasons, they will appear according to ingredient to allow you to make the seasonal choices best suited to your locale.

While for some it may be impractical to grow your own vegetables, growing your own herbs is practical for just about anyone with access to sunlight for at least part of the day. If you can afford to choose products from animals that are free-range and grass-fed, you may be happier with the quality of the food and the added nutritional content. The idea that we are making informed choices about what we eat is important, but not at the expense of taste. The good news is that these ingredients tend to taste better as well. Personally, I find that the eggs from pasture-raised chickens are much tastier than their caged counterparts. The difference in taste between farm-raised fish and wild caught can be dramatic. Because I prefer the meat I eat to be fed what nature intended it to eat (as opposed to soy and corn), when I have the option I choose beef, pork and lamb from animals that are fully pastured and grass-fed. If you've forgotten how good a cool glass of milk or a fresh pat of butter can taste, the creamy, delicious, unctuous quality of dairy products from grass-fed, fully pastured cows will remind you.

I continue to use my culinary skills in the marketing and promotion of food. In my work, I've had the pleasure to talk with many people about their health concerns and the importance of quality ingredients. The good news is that more and more consumers are turning away from processed foods in favor of whole foods and fresh ingredients. The bad news is that many food manufacturers have responded to these concerns by creating more processed foods to cater to this new "healthy" lifestyle choice. I truly believe we need to reverse our assumptions that cooking and eating well is time-consuming and somehow a luxury. This is simply not true. It is our responsibility to know what is in the food we consume. I also fully acknowledge that this often presents quite a challenge. My goal as a chef and cookbook author is to simply offer you a pathway to better eating by encouraging you to know where your food comes from and prepare most of it yourself.

ABOUT THE RECIPES

I've organized the recipes in this book into five chapters, beginning with my versions of some classic dishes like eggs Benedict; followed by my original dishes, which have been divided by whether or not the recipes include seafood or meat; and concluding with a pantry section with recipes for making components of some of the dishes (such as English muffins and bacon jam). In many cases, the way the eggs are prepared can be changed according to your preference—for example, you might choose to serve the corned beef brisket hash with scrambled eggs or eggs over-easy. This is another reason why it's important to understand the basic methods for preparing the eggs to your liking.

When learning to make a dish, it's helpful to have clear, exact instructions, so I've indicated specific ingredients and steps for each dish. However, as you become more comfortable making these dishes (or if you find you'd rather include or not include certain ingredients), I want you to feel empowered to change them to suit your palate. I firmly believe that, as you make these dishes over and over again, the more comfortable you feel executing them as written, the more comfortable you will become in creating your own versions.

Inventive, interesting dishes do not necessarily have to be complicated to make. Think of these recipes as a blueprint for you to follow, but also a starting point for your own culinary creativity. My goal in developing recipes is to create a level of complexity that is intriguing to the palate yet not overly time-consuming to prepare. There are three simple steps to accomplish this.

The first step is to choose quality ingredients. Sometimes the simplest dishes are the best because they allow the quality of the food to shine. Your responsibility in preparing the meals is to gather all the elements together, buying the best ingredients possible. As a home chef, you now often have the same access to the products used by the most famous restaurants in your area. Take advantage of your local sources when possible, and don't be afraid to ask a restaurant to share their suppliers with you. It benefits professional chefs to have their local farmers succeed in business. Enjoying an amazing tomato at a local restaurant (and asking our server where it came from) led us to discover an organic farm just miles from our house.

The second step is to use restraint when composing the dish. As the saying goes, "when in doubt, leave it out." Allow your main ingredient to take center stage and don't overcomplicate the dish with sides and sauces. Like the best chefs in the world, make a conscious choice before adding any additional element to the dish. Anything you add should enhance the quality of the main ingredient.

Finally, believe in your ability to create and practice your craft. Get in the kitchen and try new recipes. There is no litmus test for being a great chef. Some of the best chefs have never attended culinary school. You have all the qualifications you need if you have the will to persevere and the enthusiasm to create great food. All of the recipes in this book can be prepared by you, alone in the kitchen. I know this because I've made them all by myself, on many occasions. But while you don't need help to prepare them, cooking and eating are truly acts of community. You might pass your partner or close friend a paring knife and a cutting board and ask them to peel the potatoes. If your guests are food lovers (as most of ours are), they might enjoy sitting at the counter while you chop and dice. The recipes I've created are about sharing great food with friends and family. I know your guests will enjoy them as much as mine do.

CHAPTER ONE
EGG BASICS

THE ANATOMY OF AN EGG

Before you wonder why it's necessary to know the basic parts of an egg other than the obvious (shell, yolk, white), let me point out that the freshness of the egg can be reflected in some of the egg's inner qualities. So unless are lucky enough to be able to trace the freshness of your eggs from laying time to consumption, here is a little additional information about how to determine freshness from the inside out.

SHELL: This is the egg's first line of defense against the entry of bacteria. The shell color depends on the type of hen that lays it, but the nutritional value of different colored eggs is virtually the same. The eggshell is very porous, with approximately 10,000 tiny holes allowing moisture and gases in and out. This is why it's important to store eggs in a covered container in your refrigerator, as leaving eggs uncovered allows them to absorb other food odors and decreases their shelf life. Check to make sure that you don't purchase eggs with cracked shells, as they should not be consumed. The strength of the shell is related to the hen's diet and age—the older the hen, the thinner the shell.

AIR CELL: Formed at the wide end of the egg between the two membranes as it cools after being laid; the fresher the egg, the smaller the air cell. As the egg ages, moisture escapes from the pores in the shell and the air cell becomes larger.

ALBUMEN: Two third of the egg's weight is albumen, more commonly known as the egg white. A cloudy white is a sign that the egg is very fresh. Albumen is actually made up of thick albumen and thin albumen. In a fresh egg, the thin albumen is just inside the membrane while the thick albumen surrounds the yolk. As the egg ages, the thick albumen becomes thinner and less distinct. The egg white contains more than half of the egg's protein.

YOLK MEMBRANE: Surrounds and holds the yolk in shape; the fresher the egg, the stronger the membrane.

YOLK: The egg's major source of vitamins and minerals, the yolk represents about a third of an egg's weight. The color of the yolk, ranging from light yellow to deep orange, depends on the hen's feed. Blood spots are caused by a rupture of one or more small blood vessels in the yolk at the time of ovulation and do not affect the safety or taste of the egg. The yolk contains a little less than half of the egg's protein.

CHALAZAE: You know those little mucous-y things on the sides of the egg yolk? Those are the chalazae. Before they upset you, you'll be pleased to know that the fresher the egg, the more prominent the chalazae. These two protein cords hold the yolk in the center of the egg. As the egg ages, the chalazae weaken and allow the egg yolk to move off center. The chalazae are edible but are often strained out of custards or sauces for appearance.

GERMINAL DISK: Appearing as a slight depression or spot on the surface of the yolk, this is the entry for the fertilization of the egg. Chances are you've never eaten a fertilized egg, because nearly all eggs sold commercially are produced by hens that have not mated with a rooster.

SHELL MEMBRANE: The egg's second line of defense against bacteria, there are two membranes on the inside of the shell—the one that sticks to the shell and the other one that surrounds the albumen. In fresh eggs the albumen sticks to the inner shell membrane more strongly than it sticks to itself because of the more acidic environment of the egg. So when preparing hard-boiled eggs, the fresher the egg, the harder it will be to peel.

DECODING EGG LABELS

Some of the most confusing terms are used to label where eggs originate. Here is an explanation of what these terms actually mean:

ORGANIC

Organic egg producers are certified by the USDA, although specific regulations can differ from state to state. Chickens who produce certified organic eggs are cage-free, allowed free range inside their housing, and required to have access to the outdoors (although the amount of time outdoors is not regulated). They are fed an organic, all-vegetarian diet not treated with pesticides, herbicides or fertilizers. Their diet must also be free of antibiotics. The USDA rules do not, however, specify what type of outdoor area the animal has access to, or if it even actually goes outside. Compliance is verified.

CAGE-FREE

Eggs that are labeled cage-free come from hens that are not confined to cages and are allowed to roost freely in an open area, although typically an indoor room. They can engage in many of their natural behaviors such as walking and nesting. However, some recent studies indicate mixed results about the health of cage-free birds. While cage-free birds have more feathers and exhibit more natural behaviors, leaving chickens out of cages indoors doubles their risk of dying in captivity, commonly caused by pecking by other chickens. For this reason, cage-free birds often have their beaks trimmed to prevent them from causing harm to each other. There is no mandatory auditing.

HORMONE- AND ANTIBIOTIC-FREE

Hormones are banned for all egg-laying hens in commercial egg production in the United States. Additionally, only a small percentage of egg-laying flocks ever receive antibiotics, due primarily to use of effective vaccines and other management practices. Antibiotic-free claims can only be made by egg producers who choose not to use any antibiotics in feed or water during the growing period of pullets or while hens are laying eggs. Flocks producing certified organic eggs must be antibiotic-free by regulation.

FREE-RANGE

Free-range means cage-free plus having access to the outdoors. However, this "access" varies and may be as limited as a few small doors that lead to a screened-in porch or an area with no roof. The vast majority of free-range birds in commercial egg facilities never actually go outside. There are no restrictions regarding what they are fed and how long they spend outside. Because there is no government oversight of the term "free-range" when it comes to eggs, companies can add the labeling at their discretion.

VEGETARIAN DIET

This is a confusing claim because chickens are not naturally vegetarian, but rather are omnivores. If allowed to roam freely in pastures, chickens get most of their protein from worms, grasshoppers and other insects. Traditional farm flocks often consume the family's kitchen waste, including meat and fat. Hens that are fed a vegetarian diet are not consuming any animal by-products and by definition must be confined to restrict their diet.

OMEGA-3

These hens are typically given feed richer in omega-3 fatty acids like flaxseed, possibly leading to higher levels of omega-3s in their eggs. The USDA does not certify this, but reserves the right to audit farms that make the claim.

PASTURE-RAISED

In its truest form, being pasture-raised is as close to a chicken's chosen way of life as it gets. Pasture-raised birds spend most of their life outdoors but also have access to a barn for roosting. Many are able to eat a diet of worms, insects and grass in addition to feed but there are no regulations regarding what they are fed. (Poultry feed generally contains corn, roasted soy meal, sometimes oats or wheat, another protein source such as fish or crab meal, plus calcium and minerals.) However, there is no regulation regarding what constitutes pasture-raised and no requirements for the time spent on the pasture or the quality of the pasture. Some farms rotate their birds through different pastures to ensure a rich, varied diet, but there is nothing to ensure that the birds are not kept on the same plot of land. There is no mandatory auditing.

AMERICAN HUMANE CERTIFIED/ANIMAL WELFARE APPROVED/CERTIFIED HUMANE/ FOOD ALLIANCE CERTIFIED

These third-party auditing organizations assess egg farms according to a strict set of animal welfare guidelines and grant certification to those who meet their standards. Regulations set forth guidelines for how the chickens live and nest, what access they have to an outdoor environment and how they are fed and cared for. While beak trimming is often banned by humane groups, some experts argue that the painful manner of death caused to hens being pecked to death by other hens may be reason to restudy the matter. Experts are investigating alternate methods such as infrared, which may cause a reduction in pain for the procedure. However, recent research shows that keeping the hens in good environmental and housing conditions may offer a better solution. Each certified farm must maintain extensive records as well as provide access to the group's auditors in order to demonstrate compliance with standards. The details of each organization's standards are available on their websites.

HOW TO STORE EGGS

Because the eggshell is very porous, eggs should always be stored covered in the refrigerator. For best results, store eggs in a part of the refrigerator that maintains a consistent temperature, rather than on the door. Eggs should always be stored with the large end up, the same way they are packaged in the carton, to help the yolk remain centered.

Leftover raw egg whites and yolks should be put in airtight containers and stored in the refrigerator immediately. To prevent yolks from drying out, first cover them with a little water. Drain the water before using. Use leftover whites and yolks within one to two days. Hard-cooked eggs will last up to a week in the refrigerator. Dishes that contain eggs (such as casseroles) should be refrigerated and consumed within two to three days.

HOW TO PREPARE EGGS

Please don't skip this section! Although at first this may seem basic, it's important to revisit these methods of preparing eggs in order to ensure you are executing the techniques that yield the tastiest results possible. Even as a professional chef, I have personally learned new ideas from testing the various methods, and in some cases have changed the way I cook eggs because of it. So please be open to spending a little time on the basics. These methods of preparation will serve as the basis for preparing many of the recipes to follow. In some cases, you will need to adjust the time according to your own taste, so a little experimentation may be required.

Soft-Cooked Eggs

Soft-cooked eggs have a firm yet tender white and a runny yolk. Because you can't look inside the egg when cooking it in its shell, you must time these eggs exactly for the best results. As mentioned before, there are varying degrees of how solid the yolk is cooked based on personal preference, so some experimentation will be necessary. The French phrase "ouef mollet" or mollet egg is a variation—essentially a soft-cooked egg that is cooked for a longer period of time, but not as long as hard-cooked eggs. So, depending on your personal taste, cook the eggs less if you prefer a runny yolk and longer if you'd like the yolk slightly firm but not cooked through.

Method One: This method uses a cold-water start that yields a tender white. Because eggs started in cold water are sometimes difficult to peel, this method is best suited to serving the eggs in the shell.

Place the eggs in a deep saucepan in a single layer and add cold water to cover by one inch. Bring the water to a boil over high heat and immediately remove the pan from the heat and cover.

Allow the eggs to remain in the covered pan for three minutes for a just set egg white and runny yolk or up to five minutes for a firmer white and soft yolk.

Drain the eggs and rinse them under cold water for 30–60 seconds. To serve in the shell, snip off the narrow end and use a small spoon to scoop out the white and yolk.

Method Two: This method starts the eggs in hot simmering water, which makes them easier to peel.

Fill a deep saucepan about halfway with water and bring the water to a boil over high heat.

Decrease the temperature so that the water reduces to a rapid simmer and gently lower the eggs into the water one at a time in a single layer.

Cook the eggs for four minutes for a just set egg white and runny yolk or up to six minutes for a firmer white with soft yolk.

Drain the eggs and rinse them under cold water for 30–60 seconds. To serve in the shell, snip off the narrow end and use a small spoon to scoop out the white and yolk. To serve out of the shell, peel each egg by gently rolling and cracking the shell on a flat surface and spoon out the egg.

To easily peel the eggs, submerge them in an ice water bath for two minutes before peeling. The peeled eggs may be reheated in boiling water for one to two minutes.

Hard-Cooked Eggs

A hard-cooked egg has both a firm white and yolk. Hard-cooked eggs should never be boiled because boiling makes them prone to overcooking. When overcooked, the protein in the white can become rubbery and a green ring may form around the yolk. (The green is caused by sulfur and iron compounds in the egg reacting on the yolk's surface, but is safe to consume.) Hard-cooked eggs in the shell can be refrigerated up to one week.

Method One: This method yields a more tender white and a more evenly cooked yolk. Place the eggs into a deep saucepan in a single layer and add cold water to cover by one inch. Bring the water to a boil over high heat. Remove the pan from the heat and cover it. Allow the eggs to remain in the covered pan for 12 minutes. Remove the eggs from the hot water and submerge them in an ice bath until they are chilled through, about 10 minutes. Peel the eggs immediately.

Method Two: This method makes the eggs easier to peel. Fill a deep saucepan with water and bring to a boil over high heat. Add the eggs to the water and lower the heat to a simmer. Cook the eggs for 11 minutes. Remove the eggs from the hot water and submerge them in an ice bath until they are chilled through, about 10 minutes. Peel the eggs immediately.

Poached Eggs

A poached egg is simmered directly in water until the white is set but the yolk is still soft. The biggest tip I can give you about poaching eggs is to be bold. Don't be afraid of the process, as it's quite simple.

Some experts advocate poaching eggs in plain water, swirling the water to form a vortex so the egg whites congeal. Others use varying amounts of vinegar in the water to help the egg whites coagulate quickly for a neater presentation. I am presenting both approaches here for you to choose from.

Typically I use the vinegar method and rinse off the cooked eggs with plain hot water before serving. I personally have never found this to taint the taste of the egg or alter the texture. But some people seem to be more sensitive to the vinegar. If you are one of them, the plain water approach is the way to go.

If you need to hold the poached eggs using either method (for example, if you are serving a large number of people or you are reluctant to cook the eggs "live"), remove the eggs from the poaching liquid one minute before they are cooked to the desired degree of doneness. Immediately transfer the eggs to a bowl filled with cold water. To reheat the eggs, bring a large saucepan filled with water to a simmer. Gently spoon the eggs into the hot water and let them cook for one minute. Remove the eggs with a slotted spoon. Drain off the excess water and blot the egg with a paper towel to serve.

If you are using poaching cups, your eggs are actually closer to being "coddled" rather than poached, as they don't come into direct contact with the water. Coddling eggs takes a little longer but yields a tender egg white with a runny yolk (see methods below).

Method One: This is the vinegar-free method.

Use a medium skillet for four eggs or less. For more, use a large skillet, as it's important to not crowd the eggs. Fill the skillet with about 2 ½ inches of water and bring the water to a boil. Lower the heat until the water is at a gentle simmer. Take a spoon and swirl it around the inner edge of the pan a few times to create a whirlpool effect. Work quickly to get the eggs into the water while the water is still swirling. (At this point, you can crack the eggs into a ramekin and drain off any watery part of the white if desired—this will eliminate some of the ragged edges on the white. Alternatively, trim the edges of the cooked white for a neater appearance.) Otherwise, crack the first egg and then hold it very close to the water to allow it to slip in gently. Continue until all eggs are added. Slide a slotted spoon under the eggs to keep them from sticking to the bottom and to collect the egg white into a ball around the yolk. Cover the pan.

Slip a slotted spoon under the first egg after three to five minutes, depending on how runny you like the yolk, and remove it from the water. Drain off the excess water and blot the egg with a paper towel to serve. Repeat in the order that the eggs were added.

Method Two: This method uses vinegar to coagulate the egg white.

Use a medium skillet for four eggs or less. For more, use a large skillet, as it's important to not crowd the eggs. Fill the skillet with about

2 ½ inches of water and ¼ cup white vinegar and bring the water to a boil. Then lower the heat until the water is at a gentle simmer. (At this point, you can crack the eggs into a ramekin and drain off any watery part of the white if desired. Alternatively, trim the edges of the cooked white for a neater appearance.) Otherwise, crack the first egg and then hold it very close to the water to allow it to slip in gently. Continue adding eggs as desired. Slide a slotted spoon under the egg to keep it from sticking to the bottom and to collect the egg white into a ball around the yolk. Simmer the eggs for three to five minutes, depending on how runny you like the yolk. Remove the eggs with a slotted spoon and rinse in hot water. Blot the eggs with a paper towel to serve.

Scrambled Eggs

Every chef seems to have an opinion about what method makes perfect scrambled eggs. I recommend you choose how to prepare scrambled eggs based on your taste preference. Some people prefer a soft, buttery texture while others prefer a firmer one. Creamy scrambled eggs typically require slow cooking over low heat, but if you are careful, you can cook them faster but still soft. To cook eggs drier, simply cook longer over low to medium heat for the best results. Here are several different methods depending on the end result you'd like to achieve. After removing the eggs from

the heat, stir in 1-2 tsps. heavy cream or crème fraiche if desired to serve. Fresh herbs like parsley or chives are also a nice complement to scrambled eggs.

Method One: This method yields a soft, small and barely formed curd.

Crack two eggs into a cold small saucepan. Heat the saucepan on low and add one tbsp. unsalted butter. Season with salt and pepper. Using a spatula or wooden spoon, stir the eggs to combine the yolks with the whites. Continue to cook for about 5–6 minutes, lifting the pan off the heat every 30 seconds for 5–10 seconds to slow the cooking while stirring constantly. When the eggs are almost cooked, remove the pan from the heat and continue stirring until soft curds are just formed.

Method Two: This slow method yields a soft small curd that is formed.

Melt one tbsp. unsalted butter in a small skillet over low heat. Whisk two eggs together and season with salt and pepper. Add the eggs to the pan and cook, stirring constantly for 8-10 minutes until curds are formed but eggs are still glossy.

Method Three: This fast method yields a soft small curd that is formed but not quite as glossy as method two. The key is taking the eggs off the heat early and allowing them to continue to cook.

Melt one tbsp. unsalted butter in a small skillet over medium heat. Whisk two eggs together and season with salt and pepper. Add the eggs to the pan and cook, stirring constantly, for three to four minutes, until curds are formed but eggs are still wet. Remove from the heat and continue stirring until eggs are glossy. If you prefer to have your eggs drier, simply extend the amount of time they are on the heat according to your preference.

Coddled Eggs

Coddling is a gentle self-steaming method of cooking an egg that produces tender cooked whites and a runny yolk, similar to a soft-cooked egg. Rather than cooking the egg in the shell, eggs are cracked into an egg coddler or ramekin, sometimes along with other ingredients (such as a tbsp. of chopped cooked meat, vegetables, heavy cream and/or grated cheese), covered and gently cooked in simmering water. The amount of time to cook the egg will vary according to the type of baking dish you use (longer for an egg coddler with a screw-on lid, less for a shallower ramekin), so some experimentation will be necessary to achieve the desired degree of doneness. In the first two methods, the eggs are cooked on the stovetop. In the third method, the covered eggs are placed into the oven in a hot water bath to coddle.

Method One: This method uses a specialized covered dish called an egg coddler to cook the egg, but an individual ramekin tightly covered with foil will also work.

Place an egg coddler or an individual (i.e. four- to six-oz.) ramekin into a medium saucepan and add cold water until the water level is about two-thirds up the side of the dish. Remove the coddler or ramekin and bring the water to a boil over high heat. Lower the heat to a simmer. Lightly butter or grease the inside of the coddler or ramekin with butter. If adding meat and/or vegetables, place them in the bottom. Crack one egg into the coddler or ramekin. If adding cream or cheese, spoon it over top. Screw on the coddler lid or cover the ramekin tightly with foil. Cook the egg for 6-10 minutes, until the whites are set and the yolks are cooked according to the desired degree of doneness. Season the egg with salt and pepper and add fresh herbs if desired to serve.

Method Two: This method uses a lid over an open ramekin to steam the egg. This is the quickest method although perhaps not technically correct, since the egg is exposed directly to the steam from the water.

Place an individual ramekin into a large skillet or saucepan (with a lid) and add cold water until the water level is about two-thirds up the side of the dish. Remove the ramekin and bring the water to a boil over high heat. Lower the heat to a simmer. Lightly butter or grease the inside of the ramekin. If adding meat and/or vegetables, place them in the bottom. Crack an egg into the ramekin. If adding cream or cheese, spoon it over top. Place the lid onto the pan. Cook the eggs for four to eight minutes, until the whites are set and the yolks are cooked according to the desired degree of doneness. Season the egg with salt and pepper and add fresh herbs if desired to serve.

Method Three: This method uses the hot water bath, sometimes referred to as a bain-marie, which surrounds the ramekin with hot water, while the egg cooks in the oven. The water bath absorbs and distributes the heat gently and evenly around the egg.

Preheat the oven to 350 degrees F. Lightly butter or grease the inside of an individual ramekin. If adding meat and/or vegetables, place them in the bottom. Crack an egg into the ramekin. If adding cream or cheese, spoon it over top. Cover the ramekin tightly with foil. Place the filled ramekin into a roasting pan or other baking dish. Pour boiling water carefully into the roasting pan until the water reaches halfway up the sides of the ramekin. Bake for 12–15 minutes, until the white is set and the yolk is cooked according to the desired degree of doneness. Season the egg with salt and pepper and add fresh herbs if desired to serve.

Baked Eggs

Baked eggs (also known as shirred eggs) are cooked in the oven and feature firm whites and soft yolks. As with coddled eggs, the amount of time to cook the egg will vary according to the type of baking dish you use (longer for a taller ramekin with a smaller diameter, shorter for a shallow crème brûlée style dish). Again, some experimentation will be required to achieve the desired degree of doneness. Baked eggs are sometimes cooked uncovered in a hot water bath (if the eggs are covered, technically these eggs are actually coddled—see above), as this gentler method of cooking yields a softer, tender white. Baking eggs with a moist base can mitigate the need for a water bath (for example, if the egg is baked over cooked spinach or kale or in a tomato) and an added touch of cream or cheese can also help them cook more gently. Both methods are presented below. Follow the directions above for adding meat, vegetables, cream and cheese.

Method One: This method does not use the water bath.

Preheat the oven to 350 degrees F. Lightly butter or grease an individual ramekin. Crack an egg into the ramekin. Bake for 8–10 minutes, until white is mostly set and yolk is soft. The eggs will continue to cook after they are removed from the oven. Season the egg with salt and pepper and add fresh herbs if desired to serve.

Method Two: This method uses the hot water bath, sometimes referred to as a bain-marie, which surrounds the ramekin with hot water, while the egg cooks in the oven. The water bath absorbs and distributes the heat gently and evenly around the eggs.

Preheat the oven to 350 degrees F. Lightly butter or grease an individual ramekin. Crack an egg into the ramekin. Place the filled ramekin into a roasting pan or other baking dish. Pour boiling water carefully into the roasting pan until the water reaches halfway up the sides of the ramekin. Bake for 10–12 minutes, until white is set and the yolk is soft. Season the egg with salt and pepper and add fresh herbs if desired to serve.

Fried Eggs

There are several methods available, depending on whether oil or butter is typically used to fry the eggs, whether the egg is turned, and whether or not the edges are browned.

Method One: Over-Easy Egg

Over-easy means that the egg gets fried on both sides, but the yolk stays runny. "Over" refers to flipping the egg and "easy" refers to the doneness of the yolk. If you prefer the egg yolk cooked longer, this is referred to as eggs "over-medium" and

Egg Coddlers

"over-hard," but the method is the same. This method uses butter, although oil may be used instead.

In a medium skillet, melt one tbsp. unsalted butter over medium heat until it's foamy. Crack one-two eggs into the pan (alternately crack them into a small bowl and slide them into the pan) and lower the heat. Season with a pinch of salt and pepper and continue to cook over low heat until the whites become opaque, about two minutes. Turn the eggs and cook for one minute longer. Immediately remove the eggs from the pan to serve.

Method Two: Sunny Side-Up Egg

A sunny side-up egg is fried on only one side. The yolk is still completely liquid and the whites on the surface are barely set. This method uses butter, although oil may be used instead.

In a medium skillet, melt one tbsp. butter over medium heat until it's foamy. Crack one-two eggs into the pan (alternately crack them into a small bowl and slide them into the pan). Cook for one minute until the outer edges beginning to set. Add one tbsp. water to the pan, place the lid on and lower the heat. Cook for two to three minutes longer until yolks are set and whites are opaque.

Method Three: Oil-Fried Egg

Sometimes referred to as a Spanish fried egg, this version is basted with hot oil to cook the egg with a slightly crisp egg white and runny yolk.

Heat about ¼ inch of olive oil in a small skillet over medium-high heat. Crack an egg into a small bowl or ramekin. Carefully slip the egg into the oil and immediately turn the heat down to low. When the white is just set, tilt the pan and spoon the hot oil over the egg to cook the yolk. Cook for one to two minutes longer until the edges are slightly crisp and the white is cooked through.

CHAPTER TWO
The Classics

Now that we understand some basic methods for preparing eggs, here are some dishes developed by other people through the years that might be considered "classics." These are my original recipes using the classic dishes as a base for unique versions.

- Eggs Benedict
- Croque Madame
- Eggs Poached in Tomato Sauce
- Eggs in a Basket
- Huevos Rancheros
- Eggs in Potato Nests with Bacon
- French Omelet
- Italian Frittata
- Spanish Tortilla

Eggs Benedict

In Eggs Benedict, sautéed Canadian bacon is layered over lightly toasted English muffin halves, topped with poached eggs and drizzled with hollandaise. Here I have included my recipe for English muffins and hollandaise to accompany the poached eggs and ham. Eggs Benedict has a limitless number of variations—replace the English muffins with other toasted bread, grilled Portobello mushrooms or other grilled vegetables, substitute different types of meat or seafood for the Canadian bacon or try adding different herbs to the sauce to create a variety of interesting dishes.

 **SERVES 6**

- 3 large egg yolks
- 1 tsp. lemon juice
- ¼ cup dry white wine
- 1 tsp. chopped shallots
- ½ cup unsalted clarified butter (see Chef's Tip)
- ½ tsp. salt

- 3 English muffins, halved (see recipe p. 205)
- 1 tbsp. unsalted butter
- 6 slices Canadian bacon
- 6 large eggs
- 2 tsps. chopped chives or flat-leaf parsley (optional)

To make the hollandaise, whisk together the egg yolks and lemon juice and set aside. Place a stainless bowl over a saucepan containing barely simmering water (or use a double boiler). The water should not be touching the bottom of the bowl. Add the white wine, 3 tbsps. water and the shallots and cook until liquid is reduced to 2 tbsps. Strain out the shallots and return the liquid to the heat. Whisk in the egg yolk mixture. If at any point the eggs get too hot and start to break, remove the pan from the heat and whisk a few drops of cool water into the eggs. Continue whisking until the mixture is thickened and doubled in volume. Remove the mixture from the heat. Add a few drops of the melted butter, whisking it in quickly to blend or emulsify. Drizzle in the remaining butter, whisking continuously until it's all incorporated. Stir in the salt and keep warm.

Lightly toast the English muffin halves. Poach the eggs according to your preferred method (see p. 38). Heat 1 tbsp. butter in a large skillet over medium-high heat. Add the Canadian bacon and sauté for 30 seconds. Turn the bacon and sauté 30 seconds longer and remove from heat. Top each English muffin half with a slice of bacon. Top each with a poached egg. Spoon on the hollandaise and garnish with chives if using to serve.

Chef's Tip: To make the clarified butter, melt 12 ounces (1 ½ sticks) butter in a saucepan over low heat (or use the microwave) until the foam rises to the top of the melted butter. Skim the froth off the top and slowly pour the liquid into a measuring cup, discarding the milky solids at the bottom.

Croque Madame

Combining the comfort of a grilled cheese sandwich with the tasty flavor of eggs, this classic combination will become one of your favorite dishes to serve for guests or to enjoy on a leisurely morning at home.

 SERVES 6

- 5 tbsps. unsalted butter
- 3 tbsps. all-purpose flour
- 2 cups whole milk
- 1 cup grated Gruyère cheese
- ½ cup grated Parmesan
- Salt and freshly ground black pepper to taste
- ½ tsp. freshly grated nutmeg
- 12 (½-inch-thick) slices bread, toasted to golden brown
- 6 tsps. Dijon mustard
- 12 thin slices ham
- 6 large eggs

Melt 3 tbsps. butter in a medium saucepan over medium-high heat. Add the flour and whisk until smooth, about 1 minute. Whisk in the milk and bring to a boil. Reduce heat to a simmer and cook until mixture is thickened, about 6–8 minutes. Remove from the heat and stir in ½ cup grated Gruyère and the Parmesan until smooth. Season with salt and pepper and stir in the nutmeg. Set the sauce aside.

Preheat the broiler to high and set the rack 3-4 inches from the heat.

Place 6 slices toasted bread on the baking sheet, and spread 1 tsp. mustard over each. Top each with 2 slices ham. Divide the remaining Gruyère among the 6 pieces. Broil until cheese is melted, about 1–2 minutes. Top with remaining bread slices, then evenly pour the sauce on top of each sandwich. Broil until cheese sauce is bubbling and evenly browned, about 2–3 minutes, and remove from the oven.

Melt the remaining 2 tbsps. butter in a large skillet over medium heat. Add eggs and lower the heat. Season with a pinch of salt and pepper and continue to cook over low heat until the whites become opaque, about 2 minutes. Turn the eggs and cook for 1 minute longer. Place an egg on top of each sandwich to serve.

Eggs Poached in Tomato Sauce

In the Middle East this dish is sometimes called "Shakshuka," meaning "a mixture," while in the Mediterranean it is referred to as "Eggs in Purgatory," probably referring to the little bit of heat in the sauce. In either version eggs are poached in a seasoned, slightly spicy tomato sauce. This version of the classic is finished with crumbled cheese and fresh mint, but you can substitute your choice of cheese and herb. This dish is often served with toast or fresh bread for dipping.

 **SERVES 6**

- ¼ cup extra-virgin olive oil
- 1 cup chopped sweet onion
- 2 tsps. minced garlic
- 1 tsp. ground cumin
- ½ tsp. turmeric
- 1 tbsp. paprika
- 2 tsps. crushed red pepper
- 1 (28-oz.) can crushed or diced tomatoes, drained
- ½ cup chicken stock
- Salt and freshly ground black pepper to taste
- 6–12 large eggs (1–2 per person)
- ¾ cup crumbled feta
- 1 tbsp. chopped mint

Heat the oil in a large skillet over medium-high heat. Add the onion and cook, stirring occasionally, until soft, about 4–5 minutes. Add garlic, cumin, turmeric, paprika and crushed red pepper and stir for 30 seconds longer.

Add the tomatoes to the skillet. Stir in the chicken stock, reduce heat to medium and simmer until mixture is thickened slightly, about 20 minutes.

Remove the pan from the heat. Season the mixture with salt and pepper to taste. Make 6–12 indentations evenly around the pan to accommodate the number of eggs being served. Crack the eggs into the indentations in the sauce. Return the pan to the heat and cook for about 5 minutes, basting the eggs occasionally to cook evenly. Cover the skillet and cook until yolks are just set, about 2–3 minutes (longer for well done). Divide the sauce and eggs among 6 individual bowls. Sprinkle the feta and mint evenly over the eggs to serve.

Eggs in a Basket

Sometimes called eggs in a pocket, toad in a hole or one-eyed jack, in this classic, eggs are cooked in the hollowed-out center of a piece of toast. Good quality white sandwich bread from a bakery would be a time-saving substitute for the rustic loaf.

 SERVES 6

- 6 (½-inch-thick) slices rustic sandwich bread, lightly toasted (see recipe p. 215)
- 6 tbsps. unsalted butter
- 6 large eggs
- Salt and freshly ground black pepper

Use a 2-inch round cookie cutter (or a small juice glass) to cut a hole out of the center of each slice of bread. Melt 1 tbsp. butter in a large skillet over medium heat. Place 2 bread slices into the skillet. Divide 1 tbsp. butter among the holes of each piece. Crack an egg into each hole and cook until egg is set, about 7–8 minutes. Remove from the pan and repeat, cooking two at a time with the remaining 4 slices. Season with salt and pepper to taste to serve.

Huevos Rancheros

There are probably as many versions of this dish as there are Mexican cooks, but all combine eggs, chili sauce and tortillas. In this updated classic, chorizo-style sausage is added to refried beans and the homemade tortillas are topped with fried eggs and a savory tomato sauce. Corn tortillas may be substituted for the flour ones if authentic, homemade ones are available near you.

 **SERVES 6**

- 8–12 tbsps. extra-virgin olive oil
- 8 oz. ground chorizo (see recipe p. 219)
- ½ cup finely chopped onion
- 2 tsps. minced garlic
- 1 (15-oz.) can pinto or black beans, drained
- 1 cup chicken stock
- Salt and freshly ground black pepper
- 1 (24- to 26-oz.) can diced tomatoes, drained
- 1 jalapeño, stemmed and minced
- ¼ tsp. cayenne pepper
- 2 tsps. chili powder
- 1 tbsp. fresh lime juice
- Salt and freshly ground black pepper, to taste
- 6 flour tortillas, uncooked (see recipe p. 207)
- 6–12 large eggs (1–2 per person)
- ½ cup crumbled queso fresco or feta
- 2 tbsps. chopped fresh cilantro

Heat 2 tbsps. olive oil in a large saucepan over medium heat. Add the chorizo and ¼ cup onion. Stir, breaking up the sausage, until the onion is softened, about 4–5 minutes. Add the garlic and cook 30 seconds longer. Drain off any excess oil and return the pan to the heat. Add the beans and chicken stock and bring to a boil. Lower to a simmer and cook until mixture has thickened, about 10 minutes. Coarsely mash the beans with a potato masher or wooden spoon. Season with salt and pepper and keep warm.

Heat 3 tbsps. olive oil in a large saucepan or cast-iron Dutch oven over medium-high heat. Add the tomatoes, jalapeño, cayenne pepper, chili powder and remaining ¼ cup onion and stir until mixture is bubbling. Lower the heat to a simmer and cook, stirring often to allow the flavors to combine, about 5–7 minutes. Stir in the lime juice and season with salt and pepper. Keep warm.

Heat a large skillet over medium-high heat and brush with olive oil. Add a tortilla and cook for 30 seconds. Turn the tortilla and cook for 30 seconds longer. Repeat with the remaining tortillas, adding oil as necessary. Transfer tortillas to individual plates and fold them in half. Heat the remaining 3 tbsps. olive oil in a medium skillet over medium-high heat for six eggs (add 3 tbsps. additional oil if using a large skillet for twelve eggs). Crack eggs 1 by 1 into a small bowl or ramekin and season with salt and pepper, and then slide them into the oil. Immediately turn the heat down to low. When the whites are just set, tilt the pan and spoon the hot oil over the eggs. Cook for 1–2 minutes longer until the edges are slightly crisp and the whites are cooked through. Top each tortilla with 1–2 fried eggs and tomato sauce. Sprinkle on the cheese and cilantro and divide the beans evenly among the plates to serve.

French Omelet

The classic French omelet is one of the few dishes included here that is made to serve one, as each one needs to be prepared individually. No matter what fillings you choose or if you decide to simply sprinkle it with parsley, the technique for making an omelet is the same. I like to use a blender to aerate the eggs before cooking to make the omelet fluffy. If you don't have a blender, whisk the eggs until they are well blended. This recipe can also be used for egg whites, although you may want to add additional seasoning and herbs and use a non-stick skillet.

 SERVES 1

- 2–3 large eggs
- Salt and freshly ground black pepper
- 1 tbsp. unsalted butter, plus 1 tsp. softened
- 1 tsp. chopped flat-leaf parsley (or chives)

Blend or whisk the eggs with salt and pepper. In a small skillet, melt 1 tbsp. butter over medium heat until the foam subsides. Pour the eggs into the center of the pan and begin stirring them immediately for 30 seconds. Stop stirring, tilt the pan as necessary to cover the bottom with egg and allow the omelet to set up for 30 seconds. Remove the pan from the heat and allow it to continue cooking for 1 minute, until the top is still just glossy but set.

If adding filling, spoon the filling down the center of the omelet. Run a spatula around the edge or shake the pan to loosen the omelet. Fold a third of the omelet as if folding a letter. Invert the pan onto a plate to complete the final fold of the omelet. Brush the top with 1 tsp. softened unsalted butter and sprinkle on the parsley to serve.

Chef's Tip: Suggested fillings for an omelet include 2 tbsps. chopped blanched asparagus, smoked salmon, sautéed mushrooms, and/or your choice of grated or crumbled cheese.

French Omelet Fillings

Folding the Omelet

Plating the Omelet

Eggs in Potato Nests with Bacon

Eggs in Potato Nests with Bacon

This is a classic that is perhaps an update of another classic—eggs with bacon and hash browns. Here hash brown potato nests are baked with an egg in the middle and served with crumbled bacon. The result is a tasty, compact little dish that's perfect for buffet-style service.

 **SERVES 6**

- 3 large Russet or other white potatoes, peeled and quartered
- 1 tbsp. unsalted butter, melted
- ½ tsp. smoked paprika
- ½ tsp. salt
- ¼ tsp. cayenne pepper
- 6 large eggs
- 6 slices bacon
- 1 ½ tsps. chopped flat-leaf parsley

Cover the potatoes with cold salted water in a medium saucepan. Bring to a boil over high heat. Lower heat to a simmer and cook until just tender when pierced with a fork, about 10 minutes. Do not cook through. Drain and allow to cool.

Preheat the oven to 400 degrees F. Lightly grease 6 individual ramekins and set them on a baking sheet (alternately use large muffin tins).

Coarsely grate the potatoes. Mix in the butter, paprika, salt and cayenne pepper. Divide the potatoes evenly among the ramekins and press them against the bottoms and sides to form the nest. Bake for 15–18 minutes, until lightly browned.

Place one egg into each nest. Return to the oven and bake for 10–12 minutes, until the white is cooked through and the yolk is just set. In the meantime, sauté the bacon in a medium skillet over medium-high heat until fat is rendered and the bacon is crisp and lightly browned. Drain on paper towels and coarsely chop. Sprinkle the bacon evenly onto the potato nests (alternately serve on the side). Carefully remove the nests from the ramekins and sprinkle with parsley to serve.

Italian Frittata

Italian Frittata

Sometimes referred to as an Italian omelet, a frittata is a more rustic dish than a traditional French folded omelet. The word frittata, which derives from the Italian verb "friggere," or "to fry," simply refers to a variety of vegetables, cheese and meats covered with whisked eggs, which are fried in a skillet. Browning a frittata under the broiler is an easy method to finish cooking it instead of trying to flip it. Here some sautéed vegetables and a little Parmesan are added to flavor the frittata, but feel free to add cooked meat and other types of cheese according to taste.

SERVES 6

- 8 large eggs
- ½ tsp. salt
- ½ tsp. freshly ground pepper
- ½ cup grated Parmesan
- 1 medium zucchini, about 6-8 oz., shredded
- 1 ½ tbsps. unsalted butter
- 1 cup thinly sliced mushrooms
- ¼ cup finely chopped sweet onion
- 2 plum tomatoes, seeded and coarsely chopped
- 1 tbsp. chopped fresh basil

Preheat the broiler and place the top rack 3-4 inches away from the heat.

In a large bowl, whisk together the eggs, salt and pepper until the eggs are frothy. Stir in the cheese.

Put the zucchini onto a double layer of paper towels and press out the excess moisture. In a medium ovenproof skillet, melt the butter over medium heat. Add the zucchini, mushrooms and onion and sauté until softened, about 4-5 minutes. Pour the eggs over the vegetables. Cook, lifting with a rubber spatula to let the eggs flow underneath, until the edges are set but the middle still is loose, 3-4 minutes.

Remove from the heat and place under the broiler. Cook until the eggs are puffed and lightly browned, about 2-3 minutes or until the center is cooked through.

Remove from the oven and carefully slide the frittata out onto a plate. Sprinkle on the tomatoes and basil and slice into wedges to serve.

Spanish Tortilla

Often featured as a tapas dish, traditional Spanish tortilla consists of caramelized onions, thinly sliced potatoes and eggs. The onions and potatoes are cooked slowly over low heat and then finished with whisked eggs. Variations are endless, but may include the addition of Spanish chorizo, sautéed spinach and other vegetables.

 SERVES 6

- 7 tbsps. extra-virgin olive oil
- 1 ½ cups thinly sliced sweet onion (about 1 large onion)
- 1 tsp. salt
- ½ tsp. freshly ground pepper
- 5 medium white or Yukon gold potatoes
- 6 large eggs

Heat 6 tbsps. olive oil in a large skillet over medium heat. Add the onions, salt and pepper and lower the heat. Cook gently for 18–20 minutes, until the onions have softened and turned light brown.

In the meantime, peel and thinly slice the potatoes and season them with salt and pepper. Layer the potatoes over the caramelized onions in the skillet and cook on low heat for 25–30 minutes longer until the potatoes are cooked through and the onions are golden brown. Whisk the eggs together and stir them into the potato onion mixture. Remove from the heat.

Heat the remaining 1 tbsp. olive oil in a medium skillet (preferably non-stick) over medium heat. Add the potato/egg mixture. Smooth the top, lower the heat and cover the pan. Continue to cook for 8–10 minutes, until a crust has formed on the bottom. Take a plate and hold it over the tortilla in the skillet. Carefully flip the tortilla onto the plate and then immediately slide it back into the pan. Cook for 1 minute longer, then remove from the heat and allow it to cool before serving.

CHAPTER THREE
Simply Eggs

The recipes in this section do not contain meat or seafood and many are simple to make. Some require a little pre-planning, but time-saving substitutions and make-ahead suggestions are offered.

- Eggs with Roasted Cherry Tomatoes and Blue Cheese
- Cheese and Egg Soufflé
- Macaroni and Cheese with Eggs
- Quinoa with Tomato, Basil, Mozzarella and Eggs
- Wilted Spinach and Gorgonzola Omelet Roll
- Baked Tomato, Egg and Mozzarella in Phyllo Cups
- Potato Skins with Egg, Tomato and Brie
- Portobello Mushrooms with Basil Egg Topping
- Soft-Cooked Eggs with Chili-Infused Honey
- Mushroom Risotto with Eggs
- Eggs with Pesto, Leeks and Asparagus
- Eggs and Mushrooms in Brioche
- Asparagus and Sweet Onion Tart
- Egg Custard with Morels
- Eggs with Brioche and Caramelized Onions

Eggs with Roasted Cherry Tomatoes

Eggs with Roasted Cherry Tomatoes

In this simple recipe, eggs are served on top of sweet roasted tomatoes and may be sprinkled with crumbled blue cheese for an easy-to-prepare dish. Mixing different colors of cherry tomatoes yields a lovely presentation. Crumble some cooked bacon or pancetta over the tomatoes if desired.

 SERVES 6

- 2 pints cherry tomatoes, halved (about 3 cups)
- 2 tbsps. extra-virgin olive oil
- ¼ cup basil leaves, cut into chiffonade (see Chef's Tip below)
- ½ cup crumbled gorgonzola or other cheese (optional)
- 3 tbsps. unsalted butter
- 6 large eggs
- Salt and freshly ground black pepper

Preheat the oven to 400 degrees F. Lightly grease 6 individual ramekins or cast-iron skillets and set them on a baking sheet.

Divide the tomatoes among the 6 ramekins. Bake the tomatoes for 6 minutes, until just softened. Drain off any excess liquid. Drizzle on the olive oil and divide the fresh basil evenly among the 6 baking dishes. Divide the cheese evenly among the dishes if using and cook for 2 minutes longer, until the cheese is just melted.

In the meantime, prepare the eggs sunny side up. Melt 1 tbsp. butter over medium heat until it's foamy. Crack two eggs into the pan (alternatively, crack them into a small bowl and slide them into the pan). Cook for 1 minute until the outer edges begin to set. Add 1 tbsp. water to the pan, place the lid on and lower the heat. Cook for 2–3 minutes longer until yolk is set and egg white is opaque. Repeat until all eggs are cooked. Place an egg on top of each ramekin or skillet to serve.

Chef's Tip: Chiffonade (which translates as "made of rags" in French) is a technique for cutting delicate herbs or lettuce into thin, ribbon-like strips. To cut the basil into chiffonade, stack the basil leaves into a neat pile and roll them lengthwise into a fairly tight tube. Use a sharp chef's knife to slice across the roll, forming thin pieces resembling ribbons.

Cheese and Egg Soufflé

Blending cheeses made from sheep, goat and cow's milk yields a rich, complex flavor, but a variety of cheeses will work in this dish. Separating the yolks and whipping the egg whites results in an airy delight.

 **SERVES 6**

- 3 tbsps. finely ground fresh bread crumbs (see Chef's Tip below)
- 3 tbsps. unsalted butter
- 3 tbsps. all-purpose flour
- 1 tsp. salt
- 1 ½ cups whole milk, warmed
- ¼ cup grated Parmesan
- ¼ cup grated fontina
- ¼ cup grated young pecorino
- ¼ cup crumbled goat cheese
- 4 large egg yolks
- 6 large egg whites, at room temperature
- 2 tbsps. chopped fresh chives
- ½ cup crème fraîche (see recipe p. 224), at room temperature

Preheat the oven to 375 degrees F. Generously butter 6 individual ramekins or soufflé cups. Add ½ tbsp. bread crumbs to each ramekin and tilt side-to-side to coat the inside. Set the ramekins onto a baking sheet.

Melt the butter in a medium saucepan over medium heat. Whisk in the flour and salt and cook for 2 minutes. Whisk in half the milk until the mixture is smooth. Whisk in the remaining milk and heat the mixture just to a boil. Lower the heat and allow the mixture to thicken, about 2 minutes. Stir in the Parmesan, fontina, pecorino and goat cheeses. Whisk in the egg yolks and cook for 2 more minutes. Remove from the heat and allow the mixture to cool slightly.

Whisk the egg whites in a large bowl (or use an electric mixer) to form stiff peaks. Gently fold half of the egg whites into the milk/cheese mixture to lighten it, then fold in the remaining egg whites.. Divide the mixture among the ramekins. Run a steak knife around the edge about 1 inch deep to create a "top hat" effect; this ensures that the soufflé rises above the rim and doesn't stick. Bake for 25–30 minutes until puffed and golden brown. Stir the chives into the crème fraiche. Serve the soufflés immediately with the chive crème fraiche.

Chef's Tip: To prepare fresh bread crumbs, the simplest technique is to use a food processor (you can also hand grate them). Simply add chunks of stale bread to the food processor and pulse until crumbled.

The soufflé base may be made up to 2 hours ahead and refrigerated. To finish the preparation, allow the mixture to sit at room temperature for 10 minutes and whisk the egg whites just before you're ready to cook. If you're using the shorter ramekins and want the soufflé to achieve height, attach a lightly buttered 1 ½-inch-wide strip of aluminum foil or parchment tied with string around the top of each cup. Remove the collar just before serving.

Macaroni and Cheese with Eggs

This classic "mac and cheese" is made breakfast worthy with the addition of poached eggs. This version of macaroni and cheese can be made into innumerable variations by adding different types of firm cheeses, like cheddar or crumbled blue cheese. Crumbled bacon or pancetta would make nice additions as well.

 **SERVES 6**

- 3 tbsps. unsalted butter
- ½ cup chopped white onion
- 3 tbsps. all-purpose flour
- 2 cups whole milk
- 1 cup heavy cream
- 1 bay leaf
- 1 cup grated Gruyère cheese
- ½ tsp. freshly ground white pepper
- ½ tsp. ground nutmeg
- 8 oz. penne, cooked and drained
- 2 tsps. minced fresh thyme
- ¼ cup fresh coarsely ground bread crumbs
- 6 large eggs

Melt the butter in a medium saucepan. Add the onion and cook on low until translucent. Sprinkle on the flour and whisk continuously for 3 minutes. Add the milk and cream all at once, whisking continuously until combined. Stir in the bay leaf. Bring to a simmer, then lower heat and cook for about 25 minutes, until slightly thickened. Remove the mixture from the heat. Remove the bay leaf and discard. Stir in the cheese, pepper and nutmeg. Season with salt to taste.

Preheat the oven to 400 degrees F. Butter 6 individual ramekins.

Remove the mixture from the heat and stir in the cheese, pepper and nutmeg. Stir the penne into the cheese mixture to combine. Stir in the chopped thyme. Divide the mixture among the ramekins. Sprinkle on

the bread crumbs and place in the oven. Turn the oven down to 375 degrees F and bake for 15-20 minutes, until mixture is bubbling and the top is browned. Remove from the oven and allow to cool slightly.

In the meantime, prepare the poached eggs according to your preferred method (see p. 38). Place an egg on top of each ramekin to serve.

Quinoa with Tomato, Basil, Mozzarella and Eggs

Quinoa lovers will enjoy this sublime combination of quinoa with fresh tomatoes and mozzarella. Pressing the quinoa into a ring mold creates a lovely presentation, but if you don't have the rings, simply mound the quinoa mixture onto individual plates for serving.

 **SERVES 6**

- 1 cup red quinoa (substitute white or black if unavailable)
- 4 tbsps. extra-virgin olive oil
- 2 cups chicken or vegetable stock
- ½ tsp. salt
- 1 cup red cherry tomatoes, quartered
- 1 cup yellow cherry tomatoes, quartered
- 8 oz. fresh mozzarella, cut into ½-inch dice
- 6 large eggs
- Salt and freshly ground pepper to taste
- 12 basil leaves, cut into chiffonade
- 2 tbsps. balsamic vinegar or glaze

Rinse the quinoa thoroughly and drain in a metal sieve. Heat 1 tbsp. oil in a medium saucepan over medium-high heat. Add the quinoa and stir to coat. Add the chicken stock and salt and bring to a boil over medium-high heat. Lower the heat to a simmer and cover the pan. Cook for 15 minutes, until most of the liquid is absorbed. Remove from heat and allow the quinoa to sit for 5 minutes covered. Toss with a fork.

Combine the tomatoes with the mozzarella and remaining 2 tbsps. olive oil and toss to combine. Stir the tomato mixture into the warm quinoa and cover.

Poach the eggs according to your preferred method (see p. 38).

Season the quinoa with salt and pepper to taste and stir in the basil. Divide the mixture into 6 portions and press into the ring molds if using. Top each with an egg. Drizzle on the balsamic vinegar to serve.

Wilted Spinach and Gorgonzola Omelet Roll

Omelet rolls are easy to make and make a lovely presentation. Here, a savory filling of spinach and gorgonzola adds a sophisticated flair to a simply prepared dish. The variations are endless, although a Thai seasoned filling with pork and scallions is one of my favorites.

 **SERVES 6**

- 1 cup whole milk
- 6 large eggs
- ½ cup all-purpose flour
- ¼ cup unsalted butter, melted
- 2 tsps. chopped parsley
- 2 tbsps. extra-virgin olive oil
- 1 tsp. minced garlic
- 12 oz. baby spinach, washed and stems removed
- ½ cup crumbled gorgonzola cheese

Preheat the oven to 400 degrees F. Grease a jellyroll pan (15 ½ x 10 ½ x 1-inch). Line the pan with parchment and grease again.

Whisk the milk, eggs, flour and butter together in a mixing bowl until well combined and frothy. Stir in the parsley. Pour the mixture into the prepared pan and bake for 18–20 minutes, until the roll is slightly puffed and just set.

In the meantime, heat the oil in a large skillet over medium-high heat. Add the garlic and cook for 30 seconds. Add the spinach and cook for 2–3 minutes, until just wilted. Drain the spinach in a metal sieve and press out any excess moisture.

Remove the roll from the oven (leave the oven on). Spread the wilted spinach and gorgonzola evenly over the roll, leaving about ½ inch from the edges uncovered. Roll up the omelet without the parchment and place onto the baking sheet. Bake for 3–4 minutes, until the cheese is melted and the roll is just heated through. Slice into 6 pieces to serve.

Baked Tomato, Egg and Mozzarella in Phyllo Cups

Crisp phyllo is layered into flowerlike cups for this elegant presentation. Fresh plum tomatoes and mozzarella are a tasty traditional pairing in the easily assembled filling.

 **SERVES 6**

- 4 tbsps. unsalted butter
- 5 sheets phyllo
- 1 tbsp. chopped shallots
- 6 large eggs
- 3 plum tomatoes, sliced
- ½ cup shredded fresh mozzarella
- 2 tsps. chopped chives

Preheat the oven to 375 degrees F. Lightly grease a muffin pan for 6 large muffins.

Melt 2 tbsps. butter. Cut the phyllo sheets into quarters with a sharp knife. Cover the sheets with plastic wrap or a slightly damp towel (see tip below). Take ¼ sheet of phyllo dough and brush it lightly with the melted butter. Layer on a second sheet, slightly askew, so the corners do not meet. Brush with butter. Layer on a third sheet, also askew. Fit the layered pastry into the bottom of the muffin cup and press into the bottom to flatten, with pointed ends standing straight up. Repeat with the remaining dough to form 6 cups. Brush with any remaining melted butter and bake for 8-10 minutes until lightly browned. Cool the shells slightly in the pan, then carefully remove them to a baking sheet.

Melt the remaining 2 tbsps. butter in a medium sauté pan on medium heat. Add the shallots and sauté over low until softened but not browned, about 3-4 minutes. Whisk the eggs together and pour into the pan. Cook, stirring constantly, until eggs are glossy but still loose. Remove from the heat. Divide the eggs evenly among the cups. Place 2 tomato slices on top of each, and then sprinkle with mozzarella.

Bake for 4-5 minutes until the cheese is just melted. Sprinkle with chives to serve.

Chef's Tip: Phyllo dough is typically available frozen. The individual sheets are tissue thin so they can dry out quickly. For best results, defrost the dough in the refrigerator overnight. When you are ready to bake them, unroll the sheets on a flat surface and cover them with plastic wrap or a slightly damp towel (if the towel is too wet, the sheets will stick together). Remove only as much as you can work with quickly. Unused sheets may be rolled up, stored in a Ziplock bag and refrigerated for up to 2 weeks or refrozen for up to 2 months.

Potato Skins with Egg, Tomato and Brie

This breakfast version of potato skins was inspired by a deli that featured an array of stuffed potatoes for grab and go. The potatoes may be baked in advance while roasting or baking other items to save time. Simply refrigerate the cooled potatoes until ready to prepare, up to 3 days ahead. The reserved potato makes delicious home fries or pancakes.

 **SERVES 6**

- 3 large baking potatoes, scrubbed and dried
- 6 large eggs
- ½ tsp. salt
- ½ tsp. freshly ground pepper
- 1 tbsp. butter
- 3 plum tomatoes, thinly sliced
- 6 oz. brie, thinly sliced and cut into 1-inch pieces
- 2 tbsps. chopped flat-leaf parsley

Preheat the oven to 375 degrees F.

Prick the potatoes all over with a fork. Place the potatoes onto a baking sheet and bake for 1 to 1 ½ hours, until cooked through. Allow to cool slightly. Slice the potatoes in half and scoop out the flesh. (Reserve it for another use.) Place the potato skins onto a baking sheet and return to the oven to heat through, about 5-6 minutes.

In the meantime, whisk together the eggs, salt and pepper. Melt the butter in a medium skillet over medium heat. Pour the eggs into the pan and lower heat. Cook, stirring constantly, until eggs are glossy but still loose. Divide the egg mixture among the potato skins. Top each with slices of tomatoes. Bake the potatoes until the eggs are just set, about 5-6 minutes. Layer the brie onto each potato and continue baking until the cheese is just melted, about 2-3 minutes longer. Sprinkle with parsley to serve.

Portobello Mushrooms with Basil Egg Topping

Portobello mushrooms have a meaty texture that holds up well to grilling or broiling. They also make a perfect replacement for a muffin or bread base and turn an ordinary dish into a special treat. Removing the gills prevents them from discoloring the egg filling and turning it an unappealing grey.

 **SERVES 6**

- 6 large Portobello mushroom caps, stems and gills removed
- ⅓ cup extra-virgin olive oil
- 2 tbsps. balsamic vinegar
- 2 tbsps. unsalted butter
- 6 large eggs
- ½ tsp. salt
- ½ tsp. freshly ground pepper
- 2 tbsps. crème fraiche
- ½ cup crumbled fresh goat cheese
- 12 fresh basil leaves, cut into chiffonade
- 3 large plum tomatoes, seeded and coarsely chopped
- Preheat the grill or broiler.

Preheat the broiler and set the rack 3-4 inches from the heat. Brush the Portobello caps with oil and place them onto a baking sheet, cap side up. Broil the mushrooms for 2-3 minutes, until softened and beginning to brown. Turn the mushroom caps and broil for 2-3 minutes longer, until just cooked through and slightly tender. Drizzle on the balsamic vinegar and keep warm.

Melt the butter in a large skillet over medium heat. Whisk the eggs together with the salt and pepper and pour them into the skillet. Lower the heat and stir the eggs until glossy and just cooked through, about 8-10 minutes. Remove the eggs from the heat and stir in the crème fraiche until combined. Stir in the goat cheese and half of the basil. Divide the egg mixture evenly among the mushroom caps. Sprinkle on the remaining basil and tomatoes to serve.

Soft-Cooked Eggs with Chili-Infused Honey

Sometimes the simplest preparations yield the tastiest results. Here hot peppers and honey create contrasting flavors that highlight the simplicity of a perfectly soft-cooked egg. Choose a mild flavored honey for best results. Increase the number of chili peppers according to preference.

 **SERVES 6**

- 6–10 dried chili peppers
- 1 cup honey
- 6 large eggs

Place chili peppers into a glass jar or measuring cup. Warm the honey in a saucepan over medium heat until it is liquefied or until candy thermometer reaches 180° F. Pour the warm honey over the chilies. Allow to cool to room temperature and cover for 12–24 hours to allow the peppers to infuse. Strain the peppers out of the honey. Store the honey in a tightly covered sterilized jar in a cool dry place.

Prepare the soft-cooked eggs according to your preferred method (see p. 35) and drizzle with honey to serve.

Mushroom Risotto with Eggs

Mushroom Risotto with Eggs

What's better than a creamy mushroom risotto? A creamy mushroom risotto topped with an egg, of course. Any mushrooms will work in this dish, so feel free to mix it up. A little crumbled bacon or pancetta makes a nice addition as well.

- ⅓ cup dried porcini mushrooms
- 6–7 cups chicken stock
- 3 tbsps. extra-virgin olive oil
- ¼ cup finely chopped onion
- 1 ½ cups medium-grain Italian rice, such as carnaroli or arborio
- ½ cup dry white wine
- ⅓ cup grated Parmesan, plus 3 tbsps. Parmesan curls (see Chef's Tip below)
- 3 tbsps. unsalted butter
- 6 large eggs
- 2 tbsps. chopped parsley for garnish

In a small bowl, cover the dried mushrooms with warm water and soak for 15 minutes. Remove the mushrooms from the liquid with a slotted spoon. Drain the liquid through a fine sieve to remove any grit and reserve. Squeeze any excess liquid out of the mushrooms and thinly slice them.

Bring the chicken stock to a boil in a large saucepan, then lower to a simmer. Add the reserved liquid to the stock.

Heat the oil in a large skillet over medium heat. Add the onion and cook until soft and translucent, about 3–4 minutes. Add the rice and stir until coated. Cook for 2 minutes longer, until rice begins to make a "crackle" sound. Add the wine and reduce the heat to medium to a steady gentle bubbling. Stir the rice constantly until all the liquid is absorbed. Ladle in 1 cup of the warm stock and continue stirring until the liquid is absorbed. Continue to add warm stock, ½ cup at a time, stirring often, until the rice is creamy and just tender, about 25–30 minutes. Stir in the grated Parmesan and set aside.

Melt 1 tbsp. butter in a small skillet over medium-high heat. Add the mushrooms and cook until just heated through. Set aside.

Melt the remaining 2 tbsps. butter in a large skillet over medium-high heat. Crack the eggs into the skillet. Add 2 tbsps. water to the pan, place the lid on and lower the heat. Cook for 2-3 minutes longer until yolk is set and egg white is opaque. Remove the eggs from the heat.

Spoon the risotto into 6 mounds or into individual bowls. Evenly divide the mushrooms among the 6 servings. Top each mound with an egg and sprinkle on the Parmesan curls and parsley to serve.

Chef's Tip: To create the Parmesan curls, use a cheese plane or vegetable peel to slice thin strips from the block of cheese.

Eggs with Pesto, Leeks and Asparagus

A savory blend of scrambled eggs, leeks and asparagus is served over toasted English muffins and topped with a creamy pesto sauce. The egg mixture is also delicious served alone, over toasted brioche or as a topping on grilled Portobello mushrooms.

 **SERVES 6**

- 1 cup dry white wine
- 2 tsps. minced shallot
- 1 ½ cups heavy cream
- ¼ fresh basil pesto (see recipe p. 221)
- 2 tbsps. extra-virgin olive oil
- 2 medium leeks, white parts only, washed and coarsely chopped (see Chef's Tip below)
- ¼ tsp. minced garlic
- 2 tbsps. unsalted butter
- 6 large eggs
- ¼ tsp. salt
- ¼ tsp. freshly ground pepper
- 6 asparagus spears, trimmed, blanched and coarsely chopped
- 3 tbsps. crème fraiche
- 2 tsps. fresh basil, cut into chiffonade
- 6 English muffin halves (see recipe p. 205)

In a medium saucepan, combine the white wine and shallot over medium-high heat. Reduce the mixture to 3 tbsps. and remove from the heat. Strain the mixture through a metal sieve, reserving the liquid and discarding the shallots. Return the liquid to medium heat and add the cream. Reduce the mixture by half, until it is slightly thickened. Remove from the heat and stir in the pesto. Keep warm.

Heat 2 tbsps. olive oil in a medium skillet over medium heat. Add the leeks, lower the heat and sauté until tender but not colored, about 6–8 minutes. Add the garlic and sauté 30 seconds longer. Remove the mixture from the heat and set aside. Melt the butter in a large skillet over medium heat. Whisk the eggs together with the salt and pepper and pour them into the skillet. Lower the heat and continue stirring until the eggs are cooked but still glossy, about 8-10 minutes. Add the leeks and asparagus and cook for 1 minute longer, until just heated through. Remove from the heat and stir in the crème fraiche. Divide the mixture among the 6 English muffin halves. Spoon on the warm creamy pesto sauce and sprinkle on the fresh basil to serve.

Chef's Tip: Leeks are typically grown in sandy soil, so they require thorough cleaning before using. To prepare the leek, remove the roots completely and discard. Remove the upper green parts and reserve for making soups or stocks. Cut the remaining white piece lengthwise in half and submerge the halves in a bowl of cool water, shaking vigorously to remove any grit. Remove the leek from the water, leaving the grit behind in the bowl. If the leeks are particularly sandy, repeat the process with a clean bowl of water as many times as necessary.

To blanch the asparagus, bring salted water to a boil in a medium skillet. Add the asparagus and cook for 2–3 minutes, until the asparagus turn green but are still crisp.

Remove the asparagus and plunge them into an ice bath to stop the cooking. Allow to cool completely, drain and blot dry with paper towels.

Eggs and Mushrooms in Brioche

Eggs and Mushrooms in Brioche

A simple combination of delicious ingredients creates an elegant dish full of flavor. Brioche from a good bakery may be substituted for the home baked brioche. Alternately substitute a good quality sliced bread, although the presentation will not be as dramatic.

 SERVES 6

- 6 individual brioches (see recipe p. 211)
- 2 tbsps. unsalted butter
- 3 tbsps. chopped onion
- 1 ½ cups sliced mushrooms
- 3 tbsps. Madeira (optional)
- ½ cup heavy cream
- 2 tsps. chopped thyme
- ½ tsp. salt
- ½ tsp. freshly ground pepper
- 6 large eggs

Preheat the oven to 375 degrees F. Slice the tops off of the brioche and make a well in the center of the bottom piece. Place the bottoms and the tops (top side down) on a baking sheet and toast lightly in the oven, about 4-5 minutes.

Melt the butter in a medium skillet over medium heat. Add the onion and cook for 1 minute. Stir in the mushrooms and cook until softened, about 4-5 minutes. Stir in the Madeira if using and cook until the liquid is absorbed, about 3 minutes longer. Add the heavy cream and thyme. Cook until the cream is slightly thickened. Remove from the heat and season with salt and pepper.

Poach the eggs according to your preferred method (see p. 38).

Divide the mushrooms among the 6 brioche bottoms. Place an egg in each of the brioche. Sprinkle on the parsley. Place a "lid" gently onto each of the brioche to serve.

Asparagus and Sweet Onion Tart

Asparagus and Sweet Onion Tart

Fresh asparagus and sweet onions combine in this easy-to-prepare-ahead egg tart. Choose spears of medium thickness for the best flavor and texture. The little thin spears you'll sometimes see at market are not really the youngest or "baby asparagus," but are actually a sign that harvest is over for the year. Thicker spears often require peeling to remove a tougher exterior.

 SERVES 6-8

- 1 sheet puff pastry (see recipe p. 213)
- 1 tsp. salt
- 12 asparagus spears, ends trimmed
- 2 tbsps. unsalted butter
- 2 cups sliced sweet onions
- 4 oz. goat cheese
- 3 large eggs
- 1 cup half-and-half
- ½ tsp. finely ground white pepper

Preheat the oven to 375 degrees F.

Roll out the puff pastry to approximately ¼-inch thickness to fit into a 10-inch round tart pan with a removable bottom. Trim off any excess and save for another use. Line the pastry with parchment or aluminum foil and add pie weights (or use dried beans). Bake for 15 minutes, pressing down with a spatula if necessary to keep the pastry from puffing up. Remove the pastry but leave the oven on.

In the meantime, fill a large skillet with water and add ½ tsp. salt. Bring the water to a boil over medium high heat. Add the asparagus and cook until bright green and slightly tender, about 3-4 minutes. Immediately drain the asparagus and submerge them in ice-cold water. Allow the asparagus to cool through, then drain the water and set aside.

Melt the butter in a large skillet over medium heat. Add the onions and cook until softened and just beginning to turn golden, about 10-12 minutes. Spread the onions over the bottom of the tart shell. Lay the asparagus in a circular arrangement (like the spokes of a wheel) evenly over the onions. Crumble the goat cheese over the asparagus. Whisk together the eggs, half-and-half, pepper and remaining ½ tsp. salt in a large mixing bowl and pour into the crust. Bake for 20-25 minutes, until set and just beginning to brown. Cool slightly before slicing to serve.

Egg Custard with Morels

Wild morel mushrooms are available in the springtime in northern areas of the U.S. and are one of many foraged treasures we enjoyed while living in the Pacific Northwest. While many natives searched for their own, I always trusted my morel foraging to an expert mycologist and friend who would often bring some local black truffles around the same time. The delicious flavor of both inspired this simple custard that allows the ingredients to shine. Dried morels are available year round and may be used after reconstituting in warm water. If you don't have truffles available, a less costly alternative is to eliminate the addition of salt to the custard and sprinkle on some truffle-infused salt just before serving.

 SERVES 6

- 2 tbsps. unsalted butter
- 1 tsp. minced shallot
- 1 cup fresh morels, rinsed, drained and coarsely chopped
- 6 large eggs
- ¾ cup heavy cream
- ½ cup fresh bread crumbs
- ¼ tsp. salt
- ¼ tsp. freshly ground pepper
- 1 tsp. chopped fresh thyme
- 1 tsp. grated black truffle (optional)

Preheat the oven to 375 degrees F. Butter six individual custard cups or ramekins and set aside.

Melt the butter in a medium skillet. Add the shallot and sauté for 2-3 minutes, until softened. Add the morels and sauté for about 3-4 minutes longer, until just cooked through. Allow to cool slightly.

Whisk together the eggs and heavy cream in a medium mixing bowl. Fold in the bread crumbs, thyme, salt, pepper and mushrooms. Divide the mixture among the 6 custard cups. Place the cups in a 9 x 13-inch baking pan and pour boiling water in until it reaches halfway up the sides of the cups. Bake for 15-18 minutes, or until the custards are puffed and the centers are firm. Sprinkle black truffle evenly over the custards (if using) to serve.

Chef's Tip: If using dried morels, reconstitute them in warm water for 8–10 minutes until softened. Reserve the rehydrating liquid for another use, as it retains much of the flavor. Three oz. dried morels is the equivalent of 1 lb. fresh. For this recipe, use about 1 oz. dried.

Wild Morel Mushrooms

Eggs with Brioche and Caramelized Onions

Caramelizing onions adds a delicious, savory and sweet complexity to any dish. Naturally sweet onions yield the best results. Brioche loaf, challah or other good quality bread may be substituted for the home baked brioche loaf.

 **SERVES 6**

- 6 slices brioche loaf (see recipe p.211)
- 2 tbsps. unsalted butter
- 1 tbsp. extra-virgin olive oil
- 4 cups sliced onions
- ¼ cup crème fraiche (see recipe p. 224)
- 2 tbsps. chopped chives
- 6 large eggs

Toast the brioche until just golden and keep warm.

Melt the butter in a large skillet over medium heat. Stir in the oil. Add the onions and cook over low heat, stirring often until golden and caramelized, about 20–25 minutes. Remove from the heat and keep warm.

Whisk together the crème fraiche and chives in a small saucepan. Heat over low until just warm, about 2–3 minutes. Set aside.

Poach the eggs according to your preferred method (see p. 38).

Divide the onions evenly over the pieces of toast. Make a well in the center of each and scoop 1 of the poached eggs into the middle. Drizzle the crème fraiche evenly over the eggs to serve.

CHAPTER FOUR
Eggs with Meat

The recipes in this section contain meat, but in many cases it can be eliminated if desired.

- Baked Polenta with Eggs, Sausage and Fontina
- Corned Beef Brisket Hash with Poached Eggs and Horseradish
- Thai Fried Rice with Eggs, Pork Belly and Frizzled Leeks
- Steak, Eggs and Waffles with Chimichurri
- Spring Rolls with Eggs, Mushrooms and Sausage
- Duck Confit Hash with Eggs and Mushrooms
- Corn Pudding with Cilantro and Chorizo
- Eggs with Prosciutto, Sun-Dried Tomatoes & Chevre
- Prosciutto and Ricotta Cheese Pie
- Salami and Egg Tarts in Polenta Crust
- Gorgonzola Sausage Frittata
- Eggs with Kale and Pancetta
- Andouille Sausage Strata
- Breakfast Burritos with Chicken, Eggs and Salsa
- Breakfast Quesadillas
- Lentils with Prosciutto and Eggs
- Rolled Basil Soufflé with Roasted Red Pepper Coulis
- Ham and Brie Soufflé Roll
- Steak and Eggs with Cheese Grits
- Bacon Jam, Avocado and Egg Muffin Sandwiches
- Scrapple and Egg Hoagie

Baked Polenta with Eggs, Sausage and Fontina

This dish is inspired by an Italian specialty called polenta pasticciatta, which loosely translates as "messy polenta." It is a baked layered dish similar to lasagna except that it includes polenta instead of pasta. In this breakfast version, the layers are topped with egg and baked in the oven with delicious results. The dish may be assembled the night before without the egg and refrigerated until baking in the morning. A good quality Italian sausage from a butcher may be substituted to save time.

 SERVES 6

- 3 cups whole milk
- 1 cup grated fontina, Gruyère or young pecorino
- 1 tsp. salt
- 1 cup polenta or coarsely ground cornmeal
- 3 tbsps. unsalted butter
- ¼ teaspoon freshly ground black pepper
- ¼ cup grated Parmesan
- 5 tbsps. unsalted butter
- ¼ cup chopped onion
- 1 tbsp. all-purpose flour
- 1 tbsp. extra-virgin olive oil
- 1 lb. Italian sausage (see recipe p. 220)
- 6 large eggs
- 1 large tomato, thinly sliced (optional)

Preheat oven to 375 degrees F. Lightly grease a baking sheet and line with parchment. Lightly grease an 8 X 8-inch baking dish and set aside.

In a large saucepan, combine 2 cups milk with 2 cups water. Stir in the salt and bring the mixture to a boil over medium-high heat. Reduce the heat to a simmer. Stir in the cornmeal a little at a time, whisking constantly to prevent lumps. Cook for 12–15 minutes, until the polenta just pulls away from the sides of the saucepan but is still soft. Remove from the heat and stir in the butter, pepper and Parmesan. Spread the mixture evenly onto the baking sheet about ¼ inch thick and allow to cool.

Heat the remaining 1 cup milk just to a boil and remove from the heat. In a large saucepan, melt 2 tbsps. butter over medium heat. Stir in the onion and cook until softened, about 4–5 minutes. Add the flour and cook for 4–5 minutes, until lightly golden. Whisk the hot milk into the flour mixture and bring to a boil. Lower to a simmer and cook for 8–10 minutes, until the mixture is slightly thickened. Remove from the heat and stir in the fontina cheese.

Heat the olive oil in a medium skillet over medium-high heat. Add the sausage and sauté until just cooked through, about 5–6 minutes.

Whisk together the eggs in a medium bowl.

To assemble, slice the polenta into triangles or squares about 3 inches wide. Layer half of the polenta evenly into the bottom of the pan. Spread half of the cheese sauce over top. Spread half of the sausage over top. Repeat the layers with the remaining polenta, sauce and sausage. Layer on the tomato slices if using. Pour the eggs evenly over the top.

Bake for 40–50 minutes, until center is set and the top is golden brown. Cool slightly before slicing.

Corned Beef Brisket Hash with Poached Eggs and Horseradish

This savory hash is equally delicious topped with sunny side up eggs or eggs over-easy. Sweet potatoes may also be substituted for the Yukon gold for a delicious variation.

 **SERVES 6**

- 4 Yukon gold or white potatoes, peeled and cut into ¼-inch dice (about 4 cups)
- 1 tbsp. salt
- 3 tbsps. extra-virgin olive oil
- 1 tbsp. unsalted butter
- ½ cup chopped onion
- 12 thin slices cooked corned beef brisket, coarsely chopped
- 6 large eggs
- 1 cup crème fraiche (see recipe p. 224)
- ¼ cup grated fresh horseradish
- 1 tbsp. chopped chives

Place the potatoes into a medium saucepan, add water to cover and stir in the salt. Bring to a boil over high heat, reduce the heat to a simmer and cook until the potatoes are just tender, about 4-5 minutes. Drain the potatoes and place them into a bowl lined with paper towels to dry off any excess moisture.

Heat the olive oil and butter in large skillet over medium-high heat. Add the potatoes and cook until lightly browned, stirring often, about 5-7 minutes. Add the onion and cook until soft, about 3-4 minutes longer. Add the corned beef and cook until heated through, about 1-2 minutes. Keep warm.

Prepare the poached eggs according to your preferred method (see p. 38). Whisk together the crème fraiche and horseradish. Divide the hash among 6 plates and top each with a poached egg. Spoon on the horseradish crème fraiche and sprinkle with chives to serve.

Thai Fried Rice with Eggs, Pork Belly and Frizzled Leeks

Fried rice is flavored with fish sauce and pork belly and topped with an egg and some lightly fried strips of leek. Unlike bacon, pork belly is not brined, cured or smoked and retains a fresher pork flavor. If you can't find it, substitute pancetta, which is cured but not smoked.

 SERVES 6

- 1 medium leek, white part only
- 1 cup oil for frying
- ¾ tsp. coarse sea salt
- 7 tbsps. extra-virgin olive oil
- ¼ cup finely chopped sweet onion
- 1 tsp. minced garlic
- 1 tbsp. fish sauce
- 1 tsp. minced fresh ginger
- 1 lb. cooked pork belly, cut into ¼-inch dice
- 3 cups cooked rice, at room temperature
- 6 large eggs
- 1 tbsp. lime juice
- 3 scallions, trimmed and coarsely chopped

To make the leek, thinly slice it into 3-inch-long julienne strips. Rinse in a bowl of water to remove any grit, remove from the water with a slotted spoon and pat dry. In a small saucepan, heat the oil over medium-high heat until it's between 325 and 350 degrees F. on a candy/deep-fry thermometer. Reduce the heat to medium. Add ¼ of the leeks and fry, stirring with a metal slotted spoon until the leeks are light golden brown, 1–3 minutes. (The oil temperature will drop when you add the leeks; let it return to the starting temperature before frying the next batch.)

Lift the leeks from the oil using the slotted spoon, allow excess oil to drain off and transfer to a large plate lined with a couple of layers of paper towel. Gently shake on the paper towel and then slide the leeks onto the paper towel below it, discarding the oil-soaked top layer. Season the leeks with ½ tsp. salt and let them cool to room temperature.

Heat 5 tbsps. olive oil in a large nonstick skillet over medium heat. Add the onion and the remaining ¼ tsp. salt. Sauté until the onion begins to soften and just begin to brown, about 4–5 minutes. Stir in the garlic and cook for 30 seconds longer. Turn the heat to medium-high and stir in the fish sauce and ginger. Add the pork belly and cook for 30 seconds. Add the rice and cook until the rice is warmed through and beginning to brown, about 5 minutes. Remove from the heat and keep warm.

Heat a large skillet over medium heat and add the remaining 2 tbsps. of olive oil. Crack the eggs into the skillet and cook for 2 minutes until the whites are set. Turn the eggs and cook for 1 minute longer. Divide the rice evenly among 6 bowls and sprinkle on the lime juice. Top each with an egg and garnish with scallions to serve.

Steak, Eggs and Waffles with Chimichurri

This version of steak and eggs uses a savory waffle made with cornmeal as the base for an eggs Benedict style presentation. Instead of hollandaise, the poached eggs are topped with spicy chimichurri, a traditional Argentinian steak sauce.

SERVES 6

- 1 jalapeno, trimmed, seeded and finely chopped
- 1 tsp. minced garlic
- 1 ½ cups finely chopped Italian parsley
- 3 tbsps. finely chopped oregano
- ½ tsp. crushed red pepper
- 3 tbsps. lime juice
- 3 tbsps. extra-virgin olive oil
- Salt and freshly ground pepper
- 1 cup all-purpose flour
- 1 cup cornmeal
- 1 ½ tsps. baking powder
- 1 tsp. baking soda
- 1 tbsp. granulated sugar
- ½ tsp. salt
- 8 large eggs
- 2 cups buttermilk
- ½ cup unsalted butter, melted; plus 2 tbsps. unmelted
- 2 tbsps. extra-virgin olive oil
- 2 (8-oz.) strip steaks, filet mignons or sirloin steaks

In a medium bowl, combine the jalapeno, garlic, parsley, oregano, red pepper and lime juice. Stir in the olive oil and season with salt and pepper. Cover and refrigerate at least 2 hours or overnight. Allow the sauce to come to room temperature before serving.

Preheat a waffle iron to medium according to manufacturer's instructions. In a large bowl, sift together the flour, cornmeal, baking powder, baking soda, sugar and salt. Crack 2 eggs into small bowls, separating the yolks from the whites. Whisk the two egg yolks, buttermilk and ½ cup melted butter together in a small bowl. Stir the egg yolk mixture into the dry ingredients until just combined. In a

medium bowl, whisk the 2 egg whites to stiff peaks (or use an electric mixer). Fold the whites into the reserved batter until just combined.

Ladle the batter into the preheated waffle iron. Bake until golden brown, according to manufacturer's directions. Keep waffles warm until all are complete.

Melt the remaining 2 tbsps. butter in a large skillet (preferably cast-iron) over medium heat. Rub the oil all over the steaks and season them with salt and pepper. Add the steaks to the hot pan and cook for 3 minutes. Then turn the steaks and cook for 2-4 minutes longer to desired degree of doneness. Allow the steak to rest while the eggs poach. Poach the remaining 6 eggs according to your preferred method (see p. 38).

Divide the waffles among 6 plates. Slice the steaks into thin slices and divide the slices among the waffles. Top each with a poached egg. Divide the chimichurri sauce evenly over the eggs to serve.

Chef's Tip: The waffles may be made ahead of time and refrigerated for up to 24 hours or frozen for up to 1 month. To reheat, toast in a 325 degree F. oven directly on the rack until warmed through, about 5–7 minutes.

Spring Rolls with Eggs, Mushrooms and Sausage

Spring Rolls with Eggs, Mushrooms and Sausage

The perfect buffet item or breakfast treat for people on the go, these Vietnamese-style spring rolls combine traditional flavors for a morning treat. For easier service, they can be fried in advance and reheated in the oven just before serving.

 **SERVES 6**

- 1 oz. bean threads (cellophane noodles)
- 2 tbsps. peanut or coconut oil
- ¼ cup chopped shitakes
- 3 scallions, trimmed and coarsely chopped
- 3 oz. ground pork
- 6 large eggs
- 2 tbsps. fish sauce
- ½ tsp. minced garlic
- ½ tsp. ground black pepper
- 3 tsps. fresh chopped mint
- 3 tbsps. sugar
- 6 dried rice paper rounds
- 2 cups oil for frying

Soak the bean threads in hot water for 30 minutes. Drain them and cut them into 2-inch pieces.

Heat the peanut or coconut oil in a large skillet. Add the mushrooms, scallions and pork and sauté until meat is cooked through, about 4 minutes. Add the eggs and cook until glossy but forming curds. Remove from the heat and stir in the noodles, fish sauce, garlic and pepper. Stir in the mint. Allow the mixture to cool slightly.

Fill a large bowl with warm water. Add the sugar and stir to dissolve. Dip a piece of the rice paper into the water for 2 minutes. Turn to moisten the sheet completely. Lay the rice paper onto a damp kitchen cloth. Place about 1/6 of the filling on the bottom third of the sheet. Gently fold up the bottom over the filling, and then fold in the sides. Roll it the rest of the way up to form a cylinder. Place seam side down. Repeat until 6 rolls are formed.

Pour about 1 ½ inches of frying oil into a Dutch oven and heat to 350 degrees F. Add the rolls without crowding and fry until golden on all sides, about 5-6 minutes. Remove and drain on paper towels. Cut the rolls in half to serve.

Duck Confit Hash with Eggs and Mushrooms

Duck Confit Hash with Eggs and Mushrooms

Duck confit makes a tasty addition to traditional potato hash. This version is topped with sunny side up eggs, but poached eggs would work as well.

 **SERVES 6**

- ½ cup dried porcini mushrooms
- 4 medium Russet potatoes, peeled and cut into ½-inch dice
- 4 tbsps. unsalted butter
- ½ cup sliced shiitakes (substitute seasonal wild mushrooms such as chanterelles if available)
- 2 tsps. minced shallots
- ½ tsp. salt
- ½ tsp. freshly ground pepper
- 1 tbsp. veal demi-glace (optional)
- ½ cup heavy cream
- ¼ cup duck fat or extra-virgin olive oil
- 1 cup shredded duck confit (meat from about 3 legs)
- ¼ chopped onion
- 6 large eggs

In a small bowl, cover the dried mushrooms with warm water and soak for 15 minutes. Remove the mushrooms from the liquid with a slotted spoon. Drain the liquid through a fine sieve to remove any grit and reserve. Squeeze any excess liquid out of the mushrooms and thinly slice them.

Place the potatoes into a medium skillet and add salted water just to cover. Bring to a boil and cook for 4–5 minutes, until just tender but not falling apart. Drain and set aside.

Melt 2 tbsps. butter in a medium skillet over medium heat. Add the shitake mushrooms and shallots. Season with salt and pepper. Sauté until the mushrooms are softened, about 2–3 minutes. Stir in the rehydrated mushrooms and cook for 1 minute. Add the reserved liquid and cook until reduced in half, about 3–4 minutes longer. Stir in the demi-glace if using. Bring the mixture to a boil. Reduce the heat and simmer for 5-6 minutes, until most of the liquid is evaporated. Stir in the cream and simmer until thickened, about 3-4 minutes.

Heat the duck fat or olive oil in a large skillet over medium heat. Add the potatoes and sauté, stirring often for 4-5 minutes, until the potatoes are golden brown. Stir in the duck confit and onion. Sauté until the onions are softened and duck is heated through, about 4-5 minutes. Remove hash from the heat and keep warm.

Melt the remaining 2 tbsps. butter in a large skillet over medium-high heat. Crack the eggs into the skillet. Add 2 tbsps. water to the pan, place the lid on and lower the heat. Cook for 2-3 minutes longer until yolks are set and the egg whites are opaque. Remove the eggs from the heat.

Divide the duck hash into 6 portions. Top each with an egg and spoon on the mushroom sauce to serve.

Corn Pudding with Cilantro and Chorizo

Cornmeal blended with eggs creates a pudding-like consistency in this spicy sausage dish. Once baked, it slices into clean wedges perfect for buffet service, or it may be simply served family-style with a spoon. Fresh jalapeno adds a lively accent. A good quality chorizo sausage from a butcher may be substituted to save time.

 SERVES 6-8

- 1 tbsp. extra-virgin olive oil
- 8 oz. chorizo sausage (see p. 219)
- 1 ¼ cups whole milk
- ¼ cup unsalted butter
- 4 scallions, tips trimmed and coarsely chopped
- ¼ cup flour
- ½ tsp. salt
- ½ tsp. finely ground black pepper
- 4 large eggs
- ½ cup coarsely ground yellow cornmeal
- 1 cup cooked sweet corn
- ½ cup shredded cheddar cheese
- 2 jalapenos, seeded, stemmed and minced
- 3 tbsp. chopped fresh cilantro
- 3 plum tomatoes, seeded and coarsely chopped

Preheat the oven to 350 degrees F. Generously grease an 8- or 9-inch round cake pan (or, for family-style service, use a gratin or other table-ready dish) with butter and set aside.

Heat the olive oil in a medium skillet over medium-high heat. Add the chorizo and sauté until cooked through and lightly browned, about 4-5 minutes. Drain sausage on paper towels and set aside.

Heat the milk in a small saucepan until it just comes to a boil. In a large saucepan, heat the butter over medium heat until it's just melted. Add the scallions and cook until just soft, about 2 minutes. Stir in the flour. Add the hot milk and whisk vigorously until the mixture is well

Corn Pudding with Cilantro and Chorizo

combined. Stir in the salt and pepper. Remove from the heat and allow the mixture to cool slightly.

Whisk the eggs together in a measuring cup or small bowl. Stir the eggs into the cooled milk mixture. Whisk in the cornmeal. Fold in the sweet corn, sausage and cheese. Stir in half of the jalapeno peppers and half of the cilantro. Spoon the mixture into the prepared cake pan and bake for 25-30 minutes, until lightly browned and set in the center.

In the meantime, combine the remaining jalapeno pepper, cilantro and plum tomatoes in a small bowl. Remove the corn pudding from the oven and allow to cool slightly to cut into wedges. Serve with the tomato mixture.

Eggs with Prosciutto, Sun-Dried Tomatoes & Chevre

Eggs are gently coddled in the oven with a savory combination of Italian cured ham, cheese and tomatoes. A little goes a long way when adding flavor to coddled eggs.

 SERVES 6

- 2 tbsps. unsalted butter
- 2 tbsps. heavy cream
- 3 thin slices prosciutto, finely chopped
- ½ cup crumbled fresh goat cheese
- 2 tbsps. sun-dried tomatoes in oil, drained and finely chopped
- Salt and freshly ground pepper to taste
- 6 large eggs

Preheat oven to 350 degrees F. Lightly grease 6 individual ramekins.

Spoon 1 tsp. butter in the bottom of each ramekin. Evenly divide the cream, prosciutto, cheese and sun-dried tomatoes among the ramekins. Add an egg to each ramekin. Season with salt and freshly ground pepper.

Cover each ramekin with foil. Place each into a 9 x 13-inch baking dish. Fill the dish with boiling water halfway up the sides of the ramekins. Bake until the whites set and yolks are runny, about 12–15 minutes (eggs will continue to cook a little longer). Allow to cool slightly before serving.

Salami and Egg Tarts in Polenta Crust

Salami and Egg Tarts in Polenta Crust

This crust is a quick version of polenta that makes the tart easy to assemble. The eggs are cooked on the stovetop and then finished in the oven for a quickly prepared dish. The dish can also be made in a single tart pan and sliced into wedges to serve. Using high quality artisan salami will elevate the quality of the dish.

 **SERVES 6**

- 2 ½ cups half-and-half
- 1 tbsp. unsalted butter
- 1 ½ tsps. salt
- 1 cup polenta or coarsely ground cornmeal
- 2 tbsps. mascarpone
- 2 tsps. chopped flat-leaf parsley
- 10 large eggs
- ½ tsp. finely ground black pepper
- 1 tbsp. extra-virgin olive oil
- 2 tsps. minced shallots
- ¼ cup ricotta cheese (full fat or part skim)
- 6 oz. salami, cut into ¼-inch dice
- 3 tbsps. chopped roasted red pepper (optional)

Preheat the oven to 350 degrees F. Generously butter a 9- or 10-inch round tart pan with a removable bottom or use 6 individual tart pans with removable bottoms. Set aside.

Combine the half-and-half, butter and 1 tsp. salt in a medium saucepan and bring to a boil over medium-high heat. Whisk in the polenta a little at a time until all is combined. Lower the heat and continue cooking, stirring constantly until the mixture pulls away from the sides of the pans, about 5–6 minutes. Remove the pan from the heat and stir in the mascarpone and parsley. Divide the mixture into 6 and press it into the tart pans with the back of a spoon to form the crust. Bake for 10–12 minutes, until crust is lightly golden.

In the meantime, whisk the eggs together in a large bowl with the remaining ½ tsp. salt and the pepper and set aside. Heat the olive oil in a large skillet over low heat. Add the shallots and cook until soft, about 2 minutes. Pour in the eggs. Cook, stirring constantly, until glossy but still soft, about 4-5 minutes. Remove from the heat and stir in the ricotta and salami. Stir in the roasted red pepper if using.

Spoon the egg mixture evenly into the crusts. Bake for 6-8 minutes, until the eggs are just set. Remove from tart pans to serve.

Gorgonzola Sausage Frittata

This delicious version of frittata was always a guest favorite at our inn and is easy to prepare. Serve it with a side of fresh baby or micro greens drizzled tossed with olive oil and vinegar for a more substantial meal. A good quality Italian sausage from a butcher may be substituted to save time.

SERVES 6-8

- 2 medium red-skinned potatoes
- 1 tsp. salt
- 2 tbsps. extra-virgin olive oil
- 8 oz. Italian sausage (see recipe p. 220)
- 6 large eggs
- ½ tsp. ground black pepper
- 1 red bell pepper, stem and seeds removed, sliced into thin strips
- ¼ cup crumbled gorgonzola or other blue cheese
- ¼ cup basil leaves, sliced into chiffonade

Using a sharp knife or mandolin, cut the potatoes into thin slices. Place them into a large skillet and add enough water just to cover. Stir in ½ tsp. salt. Bring the water to a boil over medium-high heat. Cook for 4-5 minutes, until the potatoes are just tender but not falling apart. Drain and allow the potatoes to cool.

In a medium skillet, heat 1 tbsp. olive oil over medium heat. Add the sausage and cook until lightly browned and cooked through, about 4-5 minutes. Remove the sausage from the heat and drain off any excess fat.

Preheat the broiler and set the rack 3-4 inches away from the heat. In a large bowl, whisk the eggs with the remaining salt and the pepper until combined. Set aside.

In a medium ovenproof skillet, heat the remaining 1 tbsp. olive oil over medium heat. Add the bell pepper strips and sauté until soft, about 4-5 minutes. Remove the pan from the heat. Starting from the outside edge and working around, arrange the potato slices over the peppers, overlapping slightly. Continue until the bottom of the pan is

Gorgonzola Sausage Frittata

covered by overlapping potatoes. Distribute the cooked sausage and gorgonzola over the potatoes. Gently pour the eggs over all.

Cover the skillet and return to low heat. Cook until the eggs are beginning to set, about 5-6 minutes. Remove the skillet from the heat and place under the broiler. Cook until the eggs are puffed and lightly browned, about 2-3 minutes or until the center is cooked through.

Remove from the oven and carefully slide the frittata out onto a plate. Slice the frittata into wedges and sprinkle on the basil to serve.

Eggs with Kale and Pancetta

Eggs with Kale and Pancetta

Super-food kale makes a breakfast appearance in this tasty baked egg dish flavored with Italian bacon.

 **SERVES 6**

- 6 oz. thinly sliced pancetta
- 1 ½ lbs. kale, stems removed and discarded
- 3 tbsps. extra-virgin olive oil
- 1 tsp. minced garlic
- 1 tsp. crushed red pepper
- ½ cup chicken stock
- 1 tbsp. lemon juice
- 6 large eggs
- 6 tbsps. heavy cream
- 3 tsps. minced chives (optional)
- Salt and freshly ground pepper to taste

Preheat the oven to 400 degrees F. Line a baking sheet with parchment and spread out the pancetta on top. Bake for 10–12 minutes, until pancetta is crisp and lightly browned. Place the pancetta on paper towels to drain and cool. Coarsely chop or crumble the pancetta and set aside.

Lower the oven to 375 degrees F. Generously butter 6 individual ramekins or crème brûlée dishes and place them onto a baking sheet.

Slice the kale into thin ½-inch strips. Heat the olive oil in a large skillet over medium-high heat. Add the garlic and crushed red pepper and cook for 30 seconds. Add the kale and toss to coat with the oil. Add the chicken stock and bring to a simmer. Reduce the heat to medium, cover and cook for 5 minutes. Remove the lid and cook for 4–5 minutes longer, until all the liquid is evaporated. Remove from the heat and stir in the lemon juice and crumbled pancetta. Divide the mixture evenly among the 6 ramekins.

Crack one egg into each ramekin on top of the kale mixture. Bake for 8 minutes. Drizzle each ramekin with 1 tablespoon of the heavy cream. Continue cooking until eggs are just set up but yolks are still runny, 4–6 minutes more (longer for well done). Remove from the oven, sprinkle on chives if using and season with salt and pepper to serve.

Andouille Sausage Strata

Andouille Sausage Strata

Strata is a terrific dish for entertaining, as it is best assembled the night before and allowed to set up in the refrigerator overnight. In the morning, all that's left is baking it off and sitting back to enjoy the praise from your delighted guests. Substitute any good quality challah (or even French or Italian bread) for the brioche if desired. Andouille sausage adds the smoky, spicy flavor of New Orleans to this savory dish. A good quality Andouille sausage from a butcher may be substituted to save time.

 SERVES 6-8

- 2 tbsps. unsalted butter
- ½ cup chopped sweet onion
- 8 oz. Andouille sausages (see recipe p. 218)
- 5 large eggs
- 2 ½ cups heavy cream
- ½ tsp. salt
- ¼ tsp. cayenne pepper
- 1 tsp. smoked paprika
- 2 tsps. chopped fresh oregano
- 1 brioche loaf, cut into 2-inch cubes and lightly toasted (see recipe p. 211)
- 2 roasted red peppers, seeded and cut into thin strips
- 2 cups grated cheddar cheese
- ½ cup fresh bread crumbs

Preheat the oven to 325 degrees F. Lightly butter or grease an 8 x 8-inch baking pan and set aside.

In a medium skillet, melt the butter over low heat and add the onion. Cook until the onion is translucent and softened, about 8-10 minutes. Stir in the Andouille and cook for 3-4 minutes longer, until just cooked through. Remove from the heat and allow to cool.

Whisk together the eggs, cream, salt, cayenne pepper, paprika and oregano. Spread half the bread cubes over the bottom of the prepared pan. Sprinkle half of the Andouille/onion mixture over the bread. Layer on all of the red pepper strips. Sprinkle on 1 cup of the grated cheddar. Add a second layer each of bread, sausage and cheese. Pour the custard evenly over the layers. (If not baking right away, cover with foil and refrigerate until ready to use, or overnight. Remove the strata from the refrigerator while the oven preheats.) Leave the foil on and bake the strata for 45 minutes. Remove the foil and sprinkle on the bread crumbs. Bake for 12-15 minutes longer, until lightly browned and firm. Allow to cool slightly before serving.

Breakfast Burritos with Chicken, Eggs and Salsa

Seasonings traditionally combined in chorizo are blended with chicken for a spicy flavor. The homemade tortillas elevate this dish, but good quality store-bought tortillas (or even Napa cabbage or lettuce leaves) may be substituted if desired.

SERVES 6

- 2 tbsp. red pepper flakes
- 1 tsp. minced garlic
- ½ tsp. ground coriander
- ½ tsp. ground cumin
- 2 tsps. smoked paprika
- 1 ½ tsps. chopped oregano
- 1 (6–8 oz.) boneless, skinless chicken breast, cooked and shredded
- 3 tbsps. extra-virgin olive oil
- ½ cup shredded potato
- 6 scallions, ends trimmed and coarsely chopped
- ½ cup sliced mushrooms
- 8 large eggs
- ½ tsp. salt
- ½ tsp. freshly ground black pepper
- 2 tbsps. unsalted butter
- ½ cup shredded cheddar cheese
- ½ cup shredded Monterey jack cheese
- 6 large flour tortillas, cooked (see recipe p. 207)
- 1 cup fresh tomato salsa (see recipe p. 222)

Combine the red pepper flakes, minced garlic, coriander, cumin, paprika and oregano in a large bowl. Add the chicken and toss to combine. In a large skillet, heat 2 tbsps. olive oil over medium heat. Stir in the potato and cook until softened, about 4–5 minutes. Add the scallions and mushrooms and cook until softened, about 4–5 minutes longer. Add the seasoned chicken and cook until heated through, about 2–3 minutes. Remove from heat and set aside.

In a large bowl, whisk the eggs together with the salt and pepper. Melt the butter in a large skillet over medium heat. Pour in the eggs and lower the heat. Stir the mixture until the eggs are soft and glossy, about

Breakfast Burritos with Chicken, Eggs and Salsa

5–6 minutes. Stir in the cheeses until just melted and remove from the heat. Stir in the chicken mixture to combine.

Lay out 6 flour tortillas and divide the egg mixture among them. Roll the bottom up ⅓ and fold the sides in. Continue rolling the tortilla until it forms a neat package. Heat the remaining 1 tbsp. oil in a large skillet over medium-high heat. Add the burritos and cook until lightly browned, about 2–3 minutes per side. Serve with the fresh salsa.

Breakfast Quesadillas

Breakfast quesadillas may be filled with a variety of cheeses and meats or seafood. This version combines ham, goat cheese and Monterey jack with eggs in a creamy filling garnished with fresh avocado.

 **SERVES 6**

- 3 tbsps. unsalted butter
- ½ cup chopped onion
- 8 oz. boneless ham, diced
- 1 jalapeno, seeded and minced
- 8 oz. crumbled fresh goat cheese
- 8 oz. grated Monterey jack cheese
- 1 tbsp. chopped fresh cilantro
- 8 large eggs
- ½ tsp. salt
- ½ tsp. freshly ground black pepper
- 6 large tortillas, cooked (see p. 207)
- 3 tbsps. extra-virgin olive oil
- 1 avocado, peeled, pitted and diced
- 2 tsp. lime juice plus lime wedges for garnish

Melt 1 tbsp. butter in a medium skillet over medium heat. Add the onion and cook until softened and translucent, about 4-5 minutes. Remove from the heat and stir in the ham.

In a large bowl, combine the jalapeno, goat cheese, Monterey jack and cilantro. Add the onion and ham and mix to combine.

In a large bowl, whisk together the eggs with the salt and pepper. Melt the remaining 2 tbsps. butter in a large skillet over medium heat. Pour in the eggs and lower the heat. Stir the mixture until the eggs are soft and glossy, about 5-6 minutes. Stir in the ham and cheese mixture and remove from the heat. Lay out the tortillas and divide the mixture evenly among them, spooning it onto the bottom halves of the tortillas. Fold the tortillas in half to cover the filling.

Brush a large skillet with olive oil over medium heat. Place a folded quesadilla in the skillet and cook until lightly browned, about 2-3 minutes. Turn and cook on the other side until lightly browned, about 2 minutes longer. Repeat with the remaining quesadillas until all are heated through, adding oil as necessary. Toss the avocado with the lime juice and sprinkle over quesadillas. Garnish with lime wedges to serve.

Lentils with Prosciutto and Eggs

Brown lentils from Umbria make a hearty base for this delicious breakfast. Typically I use Italian blue cheese to finish the dish, but if you prefer a lighter flavor, substitute feta instead. Here I use olive oil to fry the eggs to yield a crispy edge, in keeping with the rustic nature of the dish. If you prefer a more tender egg, use the sunny side up method instead.

SERVES 6

- 6 tbsps. extra-virgin olive oil
- 6 thin slices prosciutto, coarsely chopped
- 1 tsp. minced garlic
- ½ cup finely chopped onion
- 1 carrot, peeled, trimmed and finely chopped
- 1 celery rib, finely chopped
- 2 plum tomatoes, peeled, seeded and coarsely chopped
- 1 cup brown Umbrian lentils (or use green LePuy lentils)
- 2–3 cups chicken stock
- 6 large eggs
- ½ cup crumbled gorgonzola or feta cheese
- 2 tsps. lemon juice
- Salt and freshly ground pepper to taste

Heat 2 tbsps. olive oil in a medium saucepan over medium heat. Add the prosciutto and cook for 1 minute. Add the garlic and cook for 30 seconds. Add the onion, carrot and celery and cook until softened, about 5-7 minutes. Stir in the chopped tomato and cook for 1 minute. Add the lentils and 2 cups chicken stock and bring to a boil. Lower the heat to barely a simmer. Cook uncovered, stirring occasionally, until the stock has been absorbed, about 20-25 minutes. Add additional stock as necessary until lentils are tender. Season with salt and pepper to taste and cover to keep warm.

In a large nonstick skillet, heat the remaining olive oil over medium-high heat. Crack the eggs into a bowl one at a time and add to the skillet. Turn the heat to low. When the white is just set, tilt the pan

Lentils with Prosciutto and Eggs

and spoon the oil over the eggs. Cook for 1-2 minutes longer until the edges are slightly crisp and the yolks are still runny. Remove from the heat. Stir the cheese and lemon juice into the warm lentils. Season with salt and pepper to taste. Divide the lentils into 6 portions and top with the eggs to serve.

Rolled Basil Soufflé with Roasted Red Pepper Coulis

Rolled Basil Soufflé with Roasted Red Pepper Coulis

A soufflé roll is an airy, savory jellyroll, also known as a roulade. If you are looking for the perfect blend of taste known as umami in an egg dish, look no further. The creamy filling studded with slightly salty Italian ham strikes a balance with the roasted red pepper sauce in this easy-to-make-ahead dish. Soufflé rolls are ideal for serving a crowd, since they can be assembled the night before and baked just before serving.

SERVES 6

- 2 ½ cups whole milk
- ¼ cup unsalted butter
- ½ cup all-purpose flour
- ½ tsp. salt
- ½ tsp. freshly ground pepper
- 5 large eggs, separated
- 2 tbsps. basil pesto
- 1 cup chopped roasted red peppers
- ¼ cup fresh tomato sauce
- 1 tbsp. extra-virgin olive oil
- 1 tbsp. minced shallots
- 1 ½ cups sliced shitake mushrooms
- 6 thin slices prosciutto, coarsely chopped
- 5 oz. crumbled goat cheese
- 5 oz. cream cheese
- 2 tbsps. chopped fresh basil

Preheat the oven to 350 degrees. Grease a jellyroll pan (15 ½ x 10 ½ x 1-inch), line with parchment and grease the parchment.

Heat the milk in a small saucepan until it just comes to a boil. Melt the butter in a medium saucepan over low heat. Stir in the flour, salt and pepper and cook for 2 minutes until bubbling. Whisk in the hot milk and bring to a simmer for 2 minutes. Whisk in the egg yolks and cook 1 minute longer. Remove from the heat and allow the mixture to cool, stirring occasionally.

Beat the eggs whites with a whisk (or use an electric mixer) in a medium bowl until they form stiff peaks. Carefully fold half the egg whites into the cooled milk mixture to lighten the mixture. Fold the remaining egg whites in until just combined. Stir in the pesto. Spread the mixture evenly in the prepared pan and bake for 15–20 minutes, until firm and just lightly browned.

In the meantime, combine ½ cup roasted red peppers with the tomato sauce in a food processor or blender until smooth. Set the coulis aside.

Heat the olive oil in a medium skillet over medium heat. Add the shallots and sauté for 1 minute. Add the mushrooms and sauté for 3–4 minutes, until just softened. Stir in the prosciutto and remove from the heat. Stir in the goat cheese, cream cheese and the remaining ½ cup roasted peppers.

Lay a kitchen towel on a work surface and cover it with a piece of parchment. Remove the jellyroll pan from the oven and immediately invert it onto the parchment. Roll the towel and soufflé up together, jellyroll-style, and allow the baked roll to cool slightly. (Leave the oven on.)

Unroll the egg soufflé and spread on the filling. Roll up the filled soufflé without the towel or parchment and place it on the prepared baking sheet. Cover with aluminum foil. Bake for 8–10 minutes until the cheese has melted and the soufflé roll is heated through. Reheat the coulis. Cut the soufflé roll into 1 ½-inch slices, sprinkle with basil and serve with the warm red pepper coulis.

Ham and Brie Soufflé Roll

Here is a tasty variation on the soufflé roll, studded with ham and filled with melted brie.

SERVES 6

- ¼ cup unsalted butter
- 2 ½ cups whole milk
- ½ cup all-purpose flour
- ½ tsp. ground black pepper
- 5 large eggs, separated
- ½ tsp. salt
- 8 oz. boneless ham steak, sliced into ¼-inch dice
- 6 oz. brie, thinly sliced and cut into ¼-inch pieces
- 2 tbsps. chopped fresh chives or flat leaf parsley
- 3 plum tomatoes, peeled, seeded and coarsely chopped

Preheat the oven to 350 degrees F. Grease a 15 ½ x 10 ½ x 1-inch jellyroll pan with butter or other shortening. Line the pan with parchment and grease the parchment paper with butter or other shortening. Line a baking sheet with parchment and set aside.

Heat the milk in a saucepan until it comes just to a boil. In a large saucepan, melt the butter over low heat. Stir in the flour and pepper and cook, whisking constantly to combine. Cook for 2 minutes until bubbling. Whisk in the hot milk and bring to a simmer for 2 minutes. Whisk in the egg yolks and salt and cook 1 minute longer. Remove from the heat and allow the mixture to cool, stirring occasionally.

Beat the eggs whites with a whisk (or use an electric mixer) in a medium bowl until they form stiff peaks. Carefully fold half the egg whites into the cooled milk mixture to lighten it. Fold the remaining egg whites in until just combined. Spread the mixture evenly in the prepared pan and bake for 15–20 minutes, until firm and just lightly browned.

Lay a kitchen towel on a work surface and cover it with a piece of parchment. Remove the jellyroll pan from the oven and immediately invert it onto the parchment. Roll the towel and soufflé up together, jellyroll-style, and allow the baked roll to cool slightly. (Leave the oven on.)

Unroll the egg soufflé and evenly sprinkle on the ham, brie and chives. Roll up the soufflé without the towel or parchment and place it onto the prepared baking sheet. Cover with aluminum foil. Bake for 8–10 minutes until the cheese has melted and the soufflé roll is heated through. Cut into 1 ½-inch slices and sprinkle on the chopped tomatoes. Serve warm.

Prosciutto and Ricotta Cheese Pie

My Italian grandmother used to make a pie like this for Easter breakfast in a square baking dish. I've replaced the traditional ham with prosciutto and added some Parmesan for flavor. Refrigerating the dough will allow it to rest and make it easier to roll out. The tart can be assembled the night before and baked in the morning. Using a tart pan with a removable bottom makes it easier to remove slices for serving.

- 1 ¼ cups all-purpose flour
- 1 tsp. salt
- ½ tsp. baking powder
- 5 large eggs
- ¼ cup extra-virgin olive oil
- 1 tbsp. fresh basil pesto (see recipe p. 221)
- 8 oz. thinly sliced prosciutto, coarsely chopped
- 1 cup half-and-half
- ½ tsp. finely ground black or white pepper
- ¼ grated Parmesan
- 1 cup fresh ricotta cheese

Combine the flour, ½ tsp. salt and the baking powder in a large bowl. In a measuring cup or small bowl, whisk together 2 eggs with the olive oil. Make a well in the center of the dry ingredients and pour in the egg mixture. Stir the mixture until it begins to form into dough. Place the dough onto a lightly floured surface and knead until smooth, about 1 minute. Shape the dough into a ball, cover with plastic wrap and refrigerate for at least 1 hour. When ready to make the pie, remove the dough from the refrigerator and bring to room temperature.

Preheat the oven to 350 degrees F.

Roll out the dough on a lightly floured surface, then invert it into a 9- or 10-inch tart pan with a removable bottom (alternately use a 9- or 10-inch pie pan). Trim any excess and discard. Prick the dough with a fork. Spread the pesto evenly over the bottom. Sprinkle the prosciutto evenly over the dough.

In a large bowl, whisk together the half-and-half, remaining 3 eggs, remaining ½ tsp. salt, pepper and Parmesan cheese. Pour the egg mixture over the ham. Drop the ricotta by tablespoons evenly over the egg filling. Bake for about 40–45 minutes, until the filling is set and lightly puffed. Cool slightly or refrigerate until ready to serve.

Steak and Eggs with Cheese Grits

The luxurious combination of steak and eggs is paired with creamy southern-style grits for a tasty breakfast.

 SERVES 6

- 1 ½ cups half-and-half
- 1 tsp. salt
- ¾ cup grits or coarsely ground cornmeal
- 1 cup shredded Monterey jack cheese
- 4 tbsps. unsalted butter
- 1 tsp. Tabasco sauce
- ¼ tsp. ground black pepper
- ¼ tsp. cayenne pepper
- ¼ cup chopped onion
- 1 (8-oz.) boneless steak (tenderloin or other tender cut), cut into thin 1-inch squares
- 6 large eggs

Combine the half-and-half with 1 ½ cups water in a large saucepan. Bring to a boil over high heat and stir in the salt. Whisk in the grits and lower the heat to a simmer. Cook the grits, whisking occasionally, until they are creamy and thick, 45–50 minutes. Stir in the cheese, 3 tbsps. butter, Tabasco, black pepper and cayenne pepper.

Preheat the oven to 350 degrees. Lightly grease 6 individual ramekins and set on a baking sheet.

Heat the remaining 1 tbsp. butter in a medium skillet over medium heat. Add the onion and cook until just softened, about 3–4 minutes. Add the steak and cook until just lightly browned, stirring constantly, about 1–2 minutes.

Divide the pieces of steak evenly among the ramekins. Divide the grits among the ramekins. Make an indention in the top of each. Crack an egg into each ramekin and season with salt and pepper. Bake the grits with eggs for 10–12 minutes, until the whites are set and the yolks are still runny. Remove from the oven and allow to cool slightly before serving (the eggs will continue to cook).

Bacon Jam, Avocado and Egg Muffin Sandwiches

Bacon Jam, Avocado and Egg Muffin Sandwiches

Delicious homemade English muffins are layered with sweet and smoky bacon jam, fresh tomatoes and creamy avocado and topped with an egg for this portable breakfast treat. Making the English muffins is simple and really worth the effort, but a bakery-quality English muffin may be substituted to save time.

 **SERVES 6**

- 6 English muffins (see recipe p. 205), halved
- 1 cup bacon jam (see recipe p. 225)
- 2 avocados, peeled, pitted and mashed
- 2 tbsps. lime juice
- ½ tsp. salt
- 1 large slicing tomato, cut into 6 thin slices
- 2 tbsps. unsalted butter
- 6 large eggs
- Freshly ground pepper

Lightly toast the English muffin halves in a toaster or under a broiler. Divide the bacon jam evenly among the 6 muffin bottoms. Mix the avocado with the lime juice and salt. Divide the avocado evenly among the muffins. Place a tomato slice on top of each.

Melt the butter in a large skillet over medium heat. Crack the eggs into the skillet and cook until the whites are set. Turn the eggs and cook for 1–2 minutes longer, until the yolks are set (2–3 minutes longer if you prefer a less runny yolk). Place an egg on top of each muffin and season with freshly ground pepper. Cover with the remaining muffin halves to serve.

Chef's Tip: If you prefer a less messy version, cook the eggs into a thin omelet layer and divide among the muffins to serve.

Scrapple and Egg Hoagie

Scrapple and Egg Hoagie

"Hoagie" is the Philadelphia word for a submarine sandwich or grinder. Scrapple, a pan-fried loaf consisting of pork, cornmeal, buckwheat flour and seasonings, is also a Philly tradition, having its roots in nearby PA Dutch country. Here, homemade scrapple is layered with eggs and cheese in a freshly baked roll for a tasty Philadelphia-style breakfast sandwich. This version features fresh slices of tomato instead of ketchup (perhaps a more traditional condiment for scrapple), but feel free to substitute it if you prefer. Freshly baked hoagie rolls are easy to make and so delicious, but a good bakery version may be substituted to save time.

 SERVES 6

- 6 hoagie rolls (see recipe p. 208)
- 12 thin slices provolone
- 4 tbsps. oil for frying
- 6 slices homemade scrapple (see recipe p. 216)
- ¼ cup all-purpose flour for dusting
- 6 plum tomatoes, thinly sliced
- 2 tbsps. unsalted butter
- 6-12 large eggs
- Salt and freshly ground pepper to taste

Preheat the broiler and set the rack 3-4 inches from the heat. Slice the hoagie rolls in half and place the bottom halves on a baking sheet. Arrange 2 slices of provolone on each roll. Place the rolls under the broiler for 1-2 minutes, until cheese is just melted. Remove from the oven and set aside.

Heat 2 tbsps. oil in a large skillet over medium-high heat. Lightly dust the scrapple slices with flour, shaking off any excess. Add 3 pieces of scrapple to the skillet and cook the slices for 3 minutes, until the edges are lightly browned. Turn the slices and continue cooking for 2-3 minutes, until the outside is crisp and the inside is heated through. Drain on paper towels. Wipe out the skillet and cook the remaining 3 slices of scrapple. Drain on paper towels.

Slice each piece of scrapple in half crosswise and arrange the halves on the melted cheese. Arrange the sliced tomatoes on top.

Melt the butter in a large skillet over medium heat. Crack the eggs into the skillet and cook until the whites are set. Turn the eggs and cook for 1-2 minutes longer, until the yolks are set (2-3 minutes longer if you prefer a less runny yolk). Place 1-2 eggs on top of each hoagie and season with salt and pepper to taste. Cover with the tops of the hoagie rolls to serve.

CHAPTER FIVE
EGG DISHES WITH SEAFOOD

Seafood adds an elegant flair to the breakfast table and in many cases brings added health benefits to the meal. In some of these recipes, the seafood can be eliminated completely, or meat can be substituted in its place.

- Smoked Salmon and Goat Cheese Soufflés
- Eggs with Salmon in Dill Crepes
- Smoked Salmon and Eggs with Spinach
- Mediterranean Eggs
- Custard Eggs in Potatoes with Caviar
- Crab and Eggs in Chive Crepes
- Almond-Crusted Crab Cakes with Eggs
- Smoked Trout Frittata with Potatoes, Horseradish & Chives
- Egg Pie with Roasted Garlic, Tomatoes and Eggplant
- Oven-Puffed Lobster and Brie Custards
- Lobster and Thyme Quiche
- Eggs Lobster Oscar with Tarragon Rounds
- Nested Eggs with Potato Blini and Dill Cream

Smoked Salmon and Goat Cheese Soufflés

The quality of this dish depends on using a good quality smoked salmon and fresh goat cheese or chevre. Don't let the idea of making a soufflé intimidate you. The addition of flour to the base makes these foolproof. To have the soufflés rise above the edge of the ramekins, add a collar to each one before baking (see Chef's Tip below).

SERVES 6

- 4 tbsps. unsalted butter
- 2 tsps. finely chopped shallots
- 1 cup coarsely chopped smoked salmon
- ½ cup crumbled goat cheese
- 1 ¼ cups whole milk
- ¼ cup all-purpose flour
- 4 large egg yolks
- 2 tsps. chopped fresh dill
- 1 tsp. salt
- 6 large egg whites
- ¼ cup crème fraiche (see recipe p. 224)
- Dill sprigs for garnish

Preheat the oven to 375 degrees F. Lightly butter 6 individual ramekins or soufflé cups and set them on a baking sheet.

Melt 2 tbsps. butter in a medium skillet over medium-high heat. Add the shallots and sauté until translucent, about 3 minutes. Add the smoked salmon and sauté for 1 minute. Stir in the goat cheese, remove from the heat and allow to cool slightly.

Heat the milk in a medium saucepan until it just comes to a boil, then remove from heat. In a separate medium saucepan, melt the remaining 2 tbsps. butter. Whisk in the flour and cook for 2 minutes, whisking constantly. Add the hot milk and whisk vigorously to combine. Cook until mixture thickens slightly, about 2 minutes. Whisk in the egg yolks and cook for 2 minutes longer. Remove the pan from the heat and stir in the dill and salt. Allow to cool slightly, about 5 minutes.

Whisk the egg whites in a medium bowl (or use an electric mixer) until they form stiff peaks. Stir the salmon mixture into the milk mixture. Gently fold about half the egg whites into the salmon mixture to lighten it. Fold in the remaining egg whites until just combined. Divide the soufflé mixture evenly among the 6 prepared cups. Bake for 20-25 minutes until the soufflés are puffed and golden brown and the centers are set. Serve the soufflés with crème fraiche and dill sprigs.

Chef's Tip: The soufflé base may be made up to 2 hours ahead and refrigerated. To finish the preparation, allow the base to sit at room temperature for 10 minutes and whisk the egg whites just before you're ready to cook. If you're using shorter ramekins and want the soufflé to achieve height, attach a lightly buttered 1 ½-inch-wide strip of aluminum foil (or parchment tied on with butcher's twine) around the top of each cup. Remove the collar just before serving.

For a dramatic presentation, place the soufflés on plates in front of each guest, insert tablespoons into the centers and spoon in a little of the crème fraiche. Top with a dill sprig.

Eggs with Salmon in Dill Crepes

This is one of my favorite dishes, as it brings back some very fond memories. I know I'm dating myself here, but I once prepared this dish on the Today Show—with Katie Couric! As a former television producer, it was my first time being in front of the camera instead of behind it. What better way to begin than on a live national broadcast? Thankfully Katie made me feel completely at ease and the segment rolled out perfectly. In addition to being television worthy, this was always a guest favorite.

 **SERVES 6**

- 1 cup all-purpose flour
- 9 large eggs
- 1 large egg yolk
- ¾ cup half-and-half
- 4 tbsps. fresh chopped dill
- ¾ tsp. salt
- 4 tbsps. unsalted butter, melted
- ½ cup dry white wine
- 1 tbsp. minced shallot
- ¾ cup heavy cream
- 4 oz. smoked salmon, coarsely chopped
- 2 tbsps. chopped sweet onion
- ½ tsp. ground white or black pepper
- ½ cup crème fraiche

Place the flour in a large mixing bowl and create a well in the center. In another mixing bowl or measuring cup, whisk together 1 egg, the egg yolk, half-and-half, ½ cup water, 2 tbsps. dill, ¼ tsp. salt and 2 tbsps. melted butter. Pour this mixture into the well and whisk to combine. Allow the crepe batter to rest for 30 minutes.

Heat an 8- or 9-inch crepe pan or skillet over medium-high heat. Brush the pan with a little of the remaining melted butter. Pour in ¼ cup batter and swirl the pan quickly so that the batter covers the pan thinly and evenly. Cook until the crepe loosens and the edge begins to curl, about 45 seconds. Turn the crepe over and cook for 30 seconds longer. Remove the crepe to a cooling rack. Continue until 6 crepes are completed, brushing with melted butter as necessary.

Eggs with Salmon in Dill Crepes

In a medium saucepan, heat the white wine with the shallots over medium heat until the liquid is reduced to a few tablespoons. Strain out the shallots and discard. Add the cream and continue cooking until mixture reduces and thickens, about 5–6 minutes. Set the sauce aside.

Preheat the oven to 350 degrees F. Lightly grease a baking sheet.

Heat the remaining butter in a large skillet over medium heat. Add the smoked salmon and onion and sauté for 2–3 minutes, until onion is softened and salmon is heated through. Whisk the remaining eggs together with the remaining salt and pepper. Pour the eggs into the skillet and lower the heat. Cook the mixture, stirring constantly, until the eggs are glossy but still soft, about 3–4 minutes. Remove from the heat and stir in the crème fraiche.

Divide the egg mixture evenly among the lower third of each crepe. Roll up the crepes and place them seam side down on the baking sheet. Bake the crepes for 5 minutes, until just heated through (the egg will firm up slightly). Reheat the sauce and stir in the remaining dill. Serve crepes with warm dill sauce.

Smoked Salmon and Eggs with Spinach

This is a variation of a traditional dish, eggs Florentine, which typically includes spinach as a base for poached eggs. In this version, the spinach is blended in creamy sauce to top the eggs, instead of the traditional hollandaise. At our Lancaster country inn, I made this dish with sorrel, a lemon scented perennial herb that flourishes in cool spring weather and grew like crazy in our garden there. If you have access to sorrel, by all means use it. Other tender cooked greens like beet greens or Swiss chard would work well too. Challah or other bread from a good bakery may be substituted for the brioche.

 **SERVES 6**

- 12 thin slices smoked salmon
- 10–12 oz. baby spinach, stems removed
- 2 tbsps. unsalted butter
- ¼ cup heavy cream
- 6 large eggs
- 6 slices brioche loaf (see recipe p.211)
- 3 tbsps. chopped chives (optional)

Preheat the broiler and set the rack 3–4 inches away from the heat.

Lay the smoked salmon out on 2 baking sheets and set aside.

Slice the spinach into ribbons. Melt the butter in a large skillet over medium heat. Add the spinach and cook until it just wilts, about 2–3 minutes. Remove from the heat and submerge the spinach in ice water. Drain in a sieve and press out any excess moisture. Return the pan to the heat and add the cream. Bring to a simmer and cook until the cream is slightly thickened, about 3–4 minutes. Stir in the spinach and cook 1 minute longer. Remove from the heat and keep warm.

Poach the eggs according to your preferred method (see p. 38)

Lightly toast the brioche slices under the broiler, about 20-30 seconds per side. Place the smoked salmon under the broiler and cook for 1-2 minutes, until just heated through.

Place 2 slices of smoked salmon on each slice of toasted brioche. Place a poached egg on top of each. Divide the spinach sauce among the 6 servings and garnish with chives if desired to serve.

Mediterranean Eggs

Tapenade, the zesty Provencal spread of olives, garlic and anchovy, inspired this savory dish with eggplant. If smaller eggplants are available, the eggplant mixture can actually be baked and served in the skins for a dramatic presentation. If you choose to eliminate the anchovies, this dish will include only vegetables.

 **SERVES 6**

- 1 large eggplant (8–10 inches long)
- 3 tbsps. extra-virgin olive oil
- 1 ½ tsps. minced garlic
- ½ cup pitted calamata olives, finely chopped
- 3 tbsps. capers, rinsed and drained
- 4 anchovy filets, rinsed and drained
- 3 plum tomatoes, peeled, seeded and coarsely chopped
- 2 tbsps. unsalted butter
- 6 large eggs
- Salt and freshly ground pepper to taste

Preheat the oven to 375 degrees F. Lightly grease a 9 x 13-inch baking dish and set aside.

Trim the ends off of the eggplant and prick it all over with a fork. Slice the eggplant in half lengthwise. Place the eggplant on a baking sheet cut side up. Bake for about 25–30 minutes or until just tender. Allow to cool slightly, then remove the flesh and discard the skin. Coarsely chop the eggplant and set aside.

Heat the oil in a large ovenproof skillet. Add the garlic and cook for 30 seconds. Add the olives, capers and anchovies and cook for 30 seconds longer. Remove the skillet from the heat and stir in the plum tomatoes and reserved eggplant. Cover the skillet with foil and bake for 15 minutes. Remove the eggplant from the oven.

Heat the butter in a large skillet over medium heat. Crack each egg into the skillet and lower the heat. Cook until the whites become opaque, about 2 minutes. Turn the eggs and cook for 1 minute longer. Divide the eggplant mixture among 6 plates and serve each with an egg. Season with salt and pepper to taste.

Custard Eggs in Potatoes with Caviar

This is another recipe that can be made without the seafood (i.e., the caviar), but it definitely adds a level of complexity to a fairly simple dish. Originally developed as egg custards baked in the empty eggshells, the extra work for presentation did not seem worthwhile, especially when intended for the breakfast table. Instead, these eggs are cooked to a custard texture using a double boiler, served in warm potatoes and topped with caviar. Another version omits the caviar and adds some fresh truffle shavings to finish the dish. However you finish them, they are tasty, beautifully presented additions to a buffet-style breakfast.

 **MAKES 18 POTATOES**

- 18 small red potatoes (each about the size of a large egg)
- 8 large eggs
- 1 ½ tsps. salt
- ½ tsp. freshly ground pepper
- 4 tbsps. unsalted butter
- 2 tbsps. crème fraiche
- 1 oz. black caviar

Preheat the oven to 325 degrees F. Line a baking sheet with parchment or foil.

Place the potatoes into a large saucepan, add water to cover and stir in 1 tsp. salt. Bring to a boil over high heat, reduce the heat to a simmer and cook until the potatoes are just tender, about 8–10 minutes (the tip of a chef's knife should easily slide into the top). Drain the potatoes and blot with paper towels to dry off any excess moisture. Slice off the tops and bottoms of the potatoes, no more than ¼ inch. (Slicing off the bottom will allow the potatoes to sit on a plate without rolling). Use a paring knife or melon baller to hollow out the top ends of the potatoes; reserve the hollowed-out potatoes for another use. Place the potatoes onto the baking sheet, season with salt and pepper and cover them with foil. Place the potatoes into the oven to heat through, about 5 minutes.

In the meantime, whisk the eggs together and season the remaining ½ tsp. salt and pepper. Place a stainless bowl over a saucepan containing barely simmering water (or use a double boiler). The water should not be touching the bottom of the bowl. Melt the butter in the bowl or top of the double boiler and swirl it around to coat the bottom. Add the eggs. Slowly scramble the eggs, stirring and folding constantly, for 10–12 minutes, until curds are loosely formed but the mixture is still very moist and loose. Remove the eggs from the heat and continue stirring for 2 minutes. Stir in the crème fraiche.

Divide the eggs among the warm potatoes and top with the caviar to serve.

Crab and Eggs in Chive Crepes

Long before the locavore movement encouraged people to eat regional foods, a fierce loyalty to the local crab existed in every coastal region of the U.S. Growing up in the Mid-Atlantic, blue crab was the crab of choice. When we lived in Maine, it was Peeky Toe. In Seattle, none could compare to Dungeness (although some King Crab from Alaska occasionally made its way to the port of Seattle). Here in Florida, the winter harvest of Stone Crab claws is eagerly anticipated every year. Whatever your favorite variety may be, treat yourself and your fellow crab lovers to this delicious breakfast.

SERVES 6

- 1 cup all-purpose flour
- 7 large eggs
- 1 large egg yolk
- ¾ cup half-and-half
- 3 tbsps. chopped chives plus whole chives for garnish
- ¼ tsp. salt
- 6 tbsps. unsalted butter, melted
- 1 tsp. minced shallot
- ½ lb. lump crabmeat
- 3 tbsps. crème fraiche (see recipe p. 224)

Place the flour in a large mixing bowl and create a well in the center. In another mixing bowl or measuring cup, whisk together 1 egg, the egg yolk, half-and-half, ½ cup water, chives, salt and 2 tbsps. melted butter. Pour this mixture into the well and whisk to combine. Allow the crepe batter to rest for 30 minutes.

Heat an 8- or 9-inch crepe pan or skillet over medium-high heat and brush the pan with 1 tsp. melted butter. Pour in ¼ cup batter and swirl the pan quickly so that the batter covers the pan thinly and evenly. Cook until the crepe loosens and the edge begins to curl, about 45 seconds. Turn the crepe over and cook for 30 seconds longer. Remove the crepe to a cooling rack. Continue until 6 crepes are completed, brushing with melted butter as necessary. Keep the crepes warm.

Poach 6 eggs according to your preferred method (see p. 38).

Heat a medium skillet over medium heat and add the remaining 2 tbsps. butter. Add the shallot and cook until just softened, about 1 minute. Add the crabmeat and cook until heated through, about 3-4 minutes. Remove from the heat and stir in the crème fraiche.

Divide the crab mixture among the 6 crepes and top each with a poached egg. Fold the crepes in half and garnish with whole chives to serve.

Smoked Trout Frittata with Potatoes, Horseradish & Chives

This lighter version of frittata with smoked trout and horseradish uses egg whites in addition to whole eggs.

 **SERVES 6**

- 2 medium red-skinned potatoes, thinly sliced
- 1 tsp. salt
- 3 large eggs
- 3 large egg whites
- ¼ cup whole milk
- ½ tsp. white pepper
- 2 tsps. extra-virgin olive oil
- 1 cup sliced sweet onions
- 1 cup smoked trout, flaked
- ¼ cup crumbled goat cheese
- 1 tbsp. freshly grated horseradish
- 1 tbsp. chopped chives

Preheat the broiler and set the rack 3–4 inches away from the heat.

In a medium skillet, cover the potatoes with cold water, add ½ tsp. salt and bring to a boil. Cook for 6–8 minutes or until just tender. Drain and cool.

In a medium bowl, whisk together the eggs, egg whites, milk, pepper and remaining ½ tsp. salt. Heat the olive oil in a medium skillet over medium heat. Add the onions and sauté for 2–3 minutes, until slightly softened. Remove from heat and arrange the potatoes overlapping over the onions. Sprinkle on the smoked trout and goat cheese. Pour the eggs over top, cover and return the skillet to low heat. Cook, lifting with a rubber spatula to let the eggs flow underneath, until the edges are set but the middle still is loose, 3–4 minutes.

Remove from the heat and place under the broiler. Cook until the eggs are puffed and lightly browned, about 2–3 minutes, or until the center is cooked through.

Remove from the oven and carefully slide the frittata out onto a plate. Sprinkle on the dill and horseradish. Cut into wedges to serve.

Almond-Crusted Crab Cakes with Eggs

Almond-Crusted Crab Cakes with Eggs

These crab cakes topped with poached eggs are an elegant breakfast entree. The dish is finished with hollandaise flavored with fresh chives.

 **SERVES 6**

- 6 tbsps. mayonnaise
- ¼ teaspoon paprika
- ⅛ teaspoon cayenne pepper
- ⅛ tsp. ground dry mustard
- ⅛ tsp. ground allspice
- 2 tsps. chopped fresh flat-leaf parsley
- ⅓ cup fresh bread crumbs
- 7 large eggs
- 1 lb. fresh lump crabmeat
- 1 tsp. paprika
- ½ cup sliced almonds
- 1 cup hollandaise (see recipe p. 223)
- 2 tsps. chopped fresh chives

Preheat the oven to 350 degrees F. Line a baking sheet with parchment and set aside.

In a medium bowl, combine 3 tbsps. mayonnaise with the paprika, cayenne pepper, mustard and allspice. Stir in the parsley and bread crumbs. Whisk 1 egg in a small bowl or measuring cup. Stir the egg into the mixture. Gently fold the crabmeat into the mayonnaise mixture. Divide the mixture into 6 and shape into crab cakes. Place the crab cakes onto the baking sheet and sprinkle with paprika.

Bake the crab cakes for 15 minutes. Remove from the oven and spoon the remaining mayonnaise evenly over the crab cakes. Divide the almonds evenly over the crab cakes and return to the oven. Bake for 4–5 minutes longer, until lightly browned.

Poach the remaining 6 eggs according to your preferred method (see p. 38) while the crab cakes finish baking. Warm the hollandaise if necessary and stir in the chives. Place a poached egg onto each of the crab cakes. Top with the chive hollandaise to serve.

Egg Pie with Roasted Garlic, Tomatoes and Eggplant

This dish combines classic Provencal flavors in a delicious tart. If the anchovies are not included, the dish becomes seafood-free. The roasted garlic and eggplant may be prepared ahead of time and stored in the refrigerator for up to 3 days.

 SERVES 8-10

- 3 large garlic heads
- 4 tbsps. extra-virgin olive oil
- 1 large eggplant, about 8–10 inches
- 1 sheet puff pastry (see recipe p. 213)
- ½ cup pitted Kalamata olives, finely chopped
- ½ cup capers, rinsed
- 6 anchovy filets, rinsed, patted dry and coarsely chopped (optional)
- 4 large eggs, hard-cooked and sliced (see p. 37)
- 5 plum tomatoes, ends trimmed and cut into thin slices
- 1 tsp. chopped fresh oregano
- 2 tbsps. grated Parmesan
- 2 tbsps. Parmesan cheese curls

Preheat the oven to 375 degrees F. Cut ¼ inch off the top of each head of garlic. Place the garlic into a shallow glass baking dish or clay garlic roaster and drizzle with 2 tbsps. oil. Cover with foil and roast garlic for 1 hour. Allow to cool slightly and then squeeze out the roasted garlic.

In the meantime, trim the ends off the eggplant and discard. Prick the skin of the eggplant all over and slice it in half lengthwise. Place the eggplant halves on a baking sheet cut side up and roast in the oven for 20–30 minutes, until completely soft. Remove from the oven and allow to cool. Scrape the pulp out into a medium bowl and discard skins. Blend the roasted garlic into the eggplant with a fork to form a paste.

Roll out the pastry to fit into a 10- 11-inch tart pan with a removable bottom. Line the shell with parchment or foil and fill with pie weights or dried beans. Bake for 10 minutes. Remove the paper and weights.

Spread the roasted garlic and eggplant into the bottom of the tart shell. Sprinkle on the olives, capers and anchovies (if using). Arrange the egg slices over the filling. Arrange the tomato slices over the egg, overlapping in a circular pattern starting with the outer edge and working in. Drizzle the remaining 2 tbsps. olive oil over the tomatoes. Sprinkle with oregano and the grated Parmesan. Bake for 20-25 minutes, until the tart is heated through and the tomatoes are lightly browned on the edges. Sprinkle on the Parmesan curls to serve.

Oven-Puffed Lobster and Brie Custards

Lobster is easy to prepare at home (see Chef's Tip below) and is one of the freshest ingredients you will ever work with. It also ends up being less expensive than you might think, because a little bit goes a long way on the breakfast table. Although there really is no substitute for lobster, all of the lobster recipes included here work well with other seafood (like crab and smoked salmon) or cooked meat (like ham or bacon), and a wide variety of cheeses according to taste.

 SERVES 6

- 6 large eggs
- ¾ cup heavy cream
- ½ cup half-and-half
- 2 tsps. chopped fresh dill
- ½ lb. cooked Maine lobster meat (about one 1 ½ lbs. lobster), coarsely chopped
- ¼ lb. brie, cut thinly into 1-inch pieces

Preheat the oven to 400 degrees F. Butter 6 individual custard cups or ramekins, place onto a baking sheet and set aside.

Whisk together the eggs, heavy cream and half-and-half in a large mixing bowl. Stir in the dill. Fill each of the cups half full with the egg mixture. Divide the lobster and brie evenly among the cups. Top each cup with the remaining egg mixture. Bake until puffed and just beginning to brown, 15–20 minutes. Serve immediately.

Chef's Tip: To cook a lobster, prepare a bowl of ice water large enough to submerge the lobster in. Bring about 2–3 inches of water to boil in a large stockpot equipped with a steamer rack. Place the lobster into the freezer for 15 minutes, and then use a chef's knife to slice down between the lobster's eyes, or alternately along the entire length of its body. This cuts through its nervous system, killing it instantly. Steam the lobster by placing it onto the rack and placing the lid on the pot. Allow the lobster to steam until just red. Immediately remove the lobster from the pot and submerge it in the ice water (this will help cool it quickly and make the meat easier to remove from the shell). Remove the claws and tail and discard the rest. To remove the meat, use a mallet or seafood cracker to break into the claws, and scissors or a chef's knife to cut down the center of the tail.

Lobster and Thyme Quiche

This quiche is made in a spring form pan or in a deep tart pan for added height and to improve the filling-to-crust ratio. If you are using a shallow quiche or tart pan, you will have enough leftover egg mixture for a second quiche. I have also made this recipe in individual tart pans for an attractive presentation. Either way, the rich filling is a satisfying, delicious breakfast entree. The quiche filling may also be prepared without the crust in a deep-dish pie pan.

 **SERVES 12-14**

- 3 cups all-purpose flour
- 2 tsps. salt
- 1 cup (16 tbsps.) unsalted butter, chilled and cut into bits
- ¼ cup finely chopped sweet onion
- 1 cup cooked Maine lobster meat, coarsely chopped
- 1 ½ cups whole milk
- 1 ½ cups heavy cream
- 4 large eggs
- ½ tsp. freshly ground white or black pepper
- 1 cup grated Gruyère
- 1 tbsp. chopped fresh thyme

In a food processor, combine the flour and 1 tsp. salt until blended. Add 14 tbsps. of the butter and pulse until just combined. Add ice water 1 tbsp. at a time and pulse until mixture is moist but still not forming a ball. Turn the mixture onto a lightly floured work surface and gather it by hand into a ball. Cover the dough with plastic wrap and place into the refrigerator for 1 hour.

Allow the dough to warm at room temperature for a few minutes before rolling.

On a lightly floured surface, roll the dough out into a large circle about 14 inches in diameter. Roll the dough up over your rolling pin and roll it out over a 9-inch spring form pan (alternatively, use a 10- to 10.5-inch diameter x 2- to 2.25-inch-deep tart pan with a removable bottom). Press the dough into the pan, allowing the crust to drape over the edge. Refrigerate the crust for 30 minutes.

Lobster and Thyme Quiche

Preheat the oven to 375 degrees F. Place the pan with the crust on a baking sheet. Line the bottom of the crust with parchment and set weights or dried beans on top. Bake the shell for 20 minutes, until the edge is lightly browned. Carefully remove the parchment and weights and continue baking for 12–15 minutes longer, until the bottom of the crust is lightly browned. Allow the crust to cool completely before filling.

Heat the remaining 2 tbsps. butter with 1 tbsp. water in a medium skillet over medium heat. Add the onion and lower the heat. Cook until the onion is transparent and softened but not browned, about 15-18 minutes. Remove from the heat and stir in the lobster meat.

Combine the whole milk, heavy cream, eggs, remaining 1 tsp. salt and pepper in a blender and blend until frothy. Add the Gruyère and thyme and blend again to combine.

Pour half of the egg cream mixture into the shell. Spoon the lobster mixture over the cream. Pour on the remaining cream to fill the shell. Bake until the custard is set and lightly browned, about 1-1 ½ hours. Allow to cool slightly before serving.

Chef's Tip: Making the quiche a day before serving and refrigerating it overnight actually improves the texture and eliminates the need to rise early. To reheat, cut the quiche into 2-inch wedges and place them on a lightly buttered parchment-lined baking sheet. Bake for 12–15 minutes in a 375 degree F. oven until heated through.

Eggs Lobster Oscar with Tarragon Rounds

Eggs Lobster Oscar with Tarragon Rounds

This dish was created during one of our summers in coastal Maine, delighting our guests, who could truly have enjoyed lobster for breakfast, lunch and dinner. Here, sautéed lobster and asparagus tips combine in the eggs Benedict style presentation. Instead of adding a traditional Béarnaise sauce, the muffin base is flavored with tarragon for a lighter touch and to allow the flavor of the lobster to really shine. The tarragon rounds may be made in advance and are delicious any time of day.

 SERVES 6

- 2 cups all-purpose flour
- 3 tbsps. cornmeal
- 2 tsps. baking powder
- ½ tsp. salt
- ½ tsp. baking soda
- ½ cup unsalted butter, plus 3 tbsps.
- ¾ cup buttermilk
- 2 tbsps. chopped fresh tarragon
- 2 tbsps. whole milk
- 1 tsp. minced shallot
- 2 tbsps. heavy cream
- 1 lb. cooked Maine lobster meat, coarsely chopped
- 6 large eggs
- 18 asparagus, peeled and blanched (see Chef's Tip)
- Salt and freshly ground pepper to taste

Preheat the oven to 450 degrees F. Line a baking sheet with parchment and lightly grease.

In a large mixing bowl, combine the flour, cornmeal, baking powder, salt and baking soda. With a pastry blender, cut in ½ cup butter until crumbly (alternatively, pulse in a food processor). Stir in the buttermilk and tarragon until just combined. Drop 2 tbsps. batter at a time onto the baking sheet to form 6 rounds. Spread the batter with the back of a spoon into 3-inch circles. Dip the spoon into the milk and smooth the tops. Bake for 12-15 minutes, until lightly browned.

Melt 2 tbsps. butter in a small skillet over medium heat. Add the shallot and cook for 1-2 minutes, until softened. Add the lobster and cream and cook for 1 minute until cream is slightly thickened and lobster is heated through. Remove from the heat.

Poach the eggs according to your preferred method (see p. 38).

Melt the remaining 1 tbsp. butter in a medium skillet over medium-high heat. Sauté the asparagus until heated through and lightly browned, about 3-4 minutes.

Divide the lobster mixture among the 6 tarragon rounds. Set 3 asparagus spears on top of each and place a poached egg on top. Season with salt and pepper to serve.

Chef's Tip: To blanch the asparagus, bring salted water to a boil in a medium skillet. Add the asparagus and cook for 2–3 minutes, until the asparagus turn green but are still crisp. Remove the asparagus and plunge them into an ice bath to stop the cooking. Allow to cool completely, drain and blot dry with paper towels.

Nested Eggs with Potato Blini and Dill Cream

This dish has a funky retro feel that makes it fun to present to guests. The egg whites can dry out a little when baked, so the dill cream adds a lovely cream touch to flavor the dish. The caviar is optional but adds a sophisticated flair. Without it, the dish does not contain seafood.

 **SERVES 6**

- 4 tbsps. crème fraiche
- 2 tbsps. chopped fresh dill
- 3 large red-skinned potatoes, scrubbed but not peeled
- 2 tsps. chopped onion
- 2 tbsps. buttermilk
- ½ tsp. salt
- ¼ tsp. cayenne pepper
- 2 large egg yolks
- 6 large eggs, separated
- 3 tbsps. oil for frying
- 2 tsps. black caviar (optional)

Preheat the oven to 375 degrees F. Line a baking sheet with parchment, lightly grease and set aside.

Combine the crème fraiche with the fresh dill in a small bowl and set aside.

To make the blini, finely grate the potatoes into a large bowl. Stir in the chopped onion, buttermilk, salt and cayenne pepper. Beat the 2 egg yolks lightly and stir them into the mixture. In a medium bowl, whisk the egg whites to stiff peaks (or use an electric mixer). Fold 3 tbsps. egg white into the potato mixture and set the remaining egg whites aside.

Heat 1 ½ tbsps. oil in a large skillet over medium heat. Divide the potato mixture into 12 even portions. Drop a portion of potato mixture into the skillet to form a blini and flatten with a spatula. Repeat to form 5 more blini. Cook until the cakes are crisp around the edges, about 1-1 ½ minutes. Turn the blini and cook the other side until lightly

Nested Eggs with Potato Blini and Dill Cream

browned, about 1-2 minutes. Drain the blini on the paper towels. Add more oil to the pan as necessary to complete 6 more blini. Keep warm.

To form the egg nests, divide the remaining egg whites into 6 small mounds on the baking sheet. Make an indentation in the center of each mound and set an egg yolk in each. Bake for 10-12 minutes, until whites are lightly browned and yolk is just set.

Place 2 blini on each plate and top with a baked egg "nest." Spoon on the dill cream and top with caviar (if using) to serve.

CHAPTER SIX
PANTRY

These are recipes for making components of some of the dishes in the previous chapters.

- English Muffins
- Flour Tortillas
- Hoagie Rolls
- Brioche
- Rustic Sandwich Bread
- Puff Pastry
- Scrapple
- Sausage
- Pesto
- Tomato Salsa
- Hollandaise Sauce
- Crème Fraiche
- Bacon Jam

English Muffins

English Muffins

Use a fork to split the muffins, rather than a knife, to create the traditional nooks and crannies.

 MAKES 6 MUFFINS

- 2 cups all-purpose flour
- 1 tbsp. granulated sugar
- ½ tsp. salt
- 1 tsp. instant yeast
- ½ tsp. baking soda
- 1 tbsp. unsalted butter, softened
- ¾ cup buttermilk
- ¼ cup cornmeal
- Coconut or other neutral oil for greasing

Mix together the flour, sugar, salt, yeast and baking soda in the bowl of an electric mixer. On low speed, mix in the butter and ¾ cup buttermilk until the ingredients form a ball. Switch to the dough hook (or knead with lightly floured hands) for 10 minutes. Form the dough into a ball, adding a little flour if necessary. Lightly grease a large bowl and place the dough ball into the bowl. Turn the dough to coat it with oil and cover with plastic wrap. Leave in a warm place to rise for about 1 ½ hours, until dough is doubled in size.

Divide the dough into 6 equal pieces with lightly floured hands. Shape the pieces into balls. Line a sheet pan with baking parchment and lightly grease the parchment. Spread half the cornmeal onto the parchment. Transfer the balls of dough to the sheet pan at least 2 inches apart. Sprinkle them loosely with the remaining cornmeal and cover the pan loosely with plastic wrap. Leave the muffins to rise in a warm place for about 1 hour longer, or until almost double in size.

Preheat the oven to 350 degrees F. Heat a skillet or griddle over medium heat and lightly brush with oil.

Uncover the muffins and gently transfer them to the skillet or griddle at least 1 inch apart. Lower the heat. Cook the muffins for 5-7 minutes, or until the bottoms are golden brown but not burnt. Turn the muffins over and cook on the other side for 5-7 minutes longer until golden brown. Immediately transfer the pieces to a sheet pan and place the pan into the oven. Bake 8-10 minutes to cook the centers (if using a digital thermometer the internal temperature should be around 200 degrees F). Transfer the baked muffins to a cooling rack and cool for at least 15 minutes before serving.

Flour Tortillas

MAKES 12 (7- TO 8-INCH) TORTILLAS

- 2 cups all-purpose flour
- ½ tsp. salt
- 1 ½ tsps. baking powder
- 2 tsps. coconut or canola oil
- 1–2 tbsps. oil for frying

In the bowl of a stand mixer equipped with a dough hook, combine flour, salt and baking powder. Add the coconut oil and ¾ cup warm water with mixer running at a medium speed, scraping down the bowl as necessary. When the mixture begins to form a ball, decrease mixing speed to low and continue to mix for 5–7 minutes, until dough is smooth.

Transfer from the mixing bowl to a well-floured work surface and divide the dough into 12 even balls. Place the dough into a baking pan and cover the pan with a damp towel. Allow the dough balls to rest for 1 hour.

On a lightly floured work surface, press each dough ball out into a 4-inch circle. With a lightly floured rolling pin, roll each dough piece into a circle about 7–8 inches in diameter (or use a tortilla press).

Heat a large skillet over medium-high heat and lightly brush with oil. Add 1 of the tortillas to the skillet and cook for 30 seconds. Turn the tortilla and cook for 30 seconds longer, until both sides have a blistered appearance. Remove to a cooling rack and repeat until all tortillas are cooked, adding oil as necessary.

Chef's Tip: Uncooked tortillas can be kept in the refrigerator, well wrapped with parchment between the layers, for up to 2 days. The tortillas may be cooked ahead and reheated when ready to serve. They may also be frozen in an airtight container for up to 1 month.

Hoagie Rolls

A simple breakfast sandwich of scrambled eggs and bacon is elevated to a higher level when served on a fresh hoagie roll (also known as a submarine or hero). These rolls are simple to make and can also be made in a variety of shapes and sizes. Divide the dough into 8 or 10 for smaller rolls if desired.

 **MAKES 6 ROLLS**

- 1 ½ tsps. instant yeast
- 2 cups all-purpose flour
- ¼ tsp. diastatic (dry) malt (optional—see Chef's Tip)
- 2 tsps. granulated sugar
- ½ tsp. salt
- 2 tbsps. canola or other neutral oil
- 3 tbsps. ground yellow cornmeal

Combine the yeast, flour, diastatic malt if using, sugar and salt in the bowl of a stand mixer. Stir in ¾ cups water at room temperature and the oil and mix until combined. Switch to the dough hook (or turn onto a lightly floured board to knead by hand) and knead for 5 minutes.

Remove the dough from the bowl and transfer it to a greased bowl. Cover with plastic wrap and allow to rise in a warm spot, until doubled in size, about 1 hour.

Divide the dough into 6 pieces with lightly floured hands and shape into logs. Line a baking sheet with parchment and lightly grease the parchment. Dust the parchment with the cornmeal. Transfer the rolls to the baking sheet. Cover loosely with plastic wrap. Allow the rolls to rise for 30 minutes, until they are puffy and almost doubled in size.

Preheat the oven to 375 degrees F. Cut a slash lengthwise on each log. Lightly mist the rolls with cool water as soon as you slide the pan into the oven. Bake the rolls for 18–20 minutes or until golden brown. Remove to wire racks to cool.

Chef's Tip: Diastatic malt contains a group of enzymes called diastase, which breaks down starch into sugars that can be acted upon by yeast. When added to bread dough, it is a powerful food for yeast and is typically used when fermentation times are short. Adding diastatic malt promotes great texture and a lovely brown crust, but it is optional.

Brioche

Brioche

Buttery brioche has a tender crumb and is a tasty base for many egg dishes. However, the smell of these baking will make it hard for you to save them for other recipes. If you don't have brioche tins, a standard muffin pan will substitute. This is a simplified version of traditional brioche for use as a component in some of the egg dishes.

 MAKES 12 INDIVIDUAL BRIOCHES OR 2 LOAVES

- ½ cup whole milk
- 8 oz. unsalted butter, in bits
- 5 tbsps. granulated sugar
- ½ tsp. salt
- 6 large eggs
- 6–6 ½ cups all-purpose flour
- 5 ½ tsps. instant yeast
- ½ tsp. salt
- 1 large egg yolk

Heat the milk just to a boil in a small saucepan over medium high heat. Remove from the heat and stir in the butter until melted. Add the sugar and salt and stir to dissolve. Allow the mixture to cool.

In the bowl of a stand mixer (or in a large bowl if mixing by hand) combine the milk with the eggs until smooth. Whisk 4 cups flour with the yeast in a separate bowl. Pour the flour and yeast into the milk mixture and mix until just combined. Add 2 cups flour and mix until just combined, scraping dough together as necessary. Switch to the dough hook or knead by hand for 10 minutes, until the dough is smooth but still sticky.

Lightly grease a large bowl. With floured hands, gather the dough into a ball. Transfer the dough to a lightly floured surface and add the remaining ½ cup flour a little at a time until the dough is able to be kneaded but remains soft. Knead for 3 minutes longer. Form the dough into a round mound and place it into the bowl. Cover the bowl loosely with plastic wrap and let it rise until about doubled, about 1 ½ hours.

Punch the dough down and transfer it to the floured work surface. Again, stretch the dough and reshape it into a round. Return the dough to the bowl and cover it with plastic wrap. Place the bowl into the refrigerator for at least 6 hours or ideally overnight. Check the dough after 2 hours and punch it down if it has doubled in size (this will depend on your refrigerator temperature and how fast the dough cools down).

Remove the dough from the refrigerator and allow it to come to room temperature. Place it on a lightly floured work surface.

If making individual brioche, lightly grease 12 individual brioche tins. Divide the dough into 14 even pieces. Shape the pieces into balls with lightly floured hands. Set 1 ball into each of the 12 brioche pans. Divide the remaining 2 balls into 6 pieces and roll each into a smaller ball. Make an indent in the top of each brioche and set 1 of the smaller balls in it to form the top knot. Set the brioche tins onto a baking sheet and cover loosely with plastic wrap. Allow to rise until doubled, about 1 hour.

If making loaves, lightly grease two 8 x 4 x 3-inch loaf pans. Divide the dough into 12 even pieces. Set 6 balls into each loaf pan, forming 2 rows of 3. Cover with plastic wrap. Allow the dough to rise until it reaches the top of the pan and all the balls are touching, about 2–2 ½ hours.

Preheat the oven to 375 degrees F. Whisk the egg yolk with 1 tsp. water and brush the tops of the brioche or loaves, being careful to not let the egg wash drip down the sides. For individual brioche, bake until golden brown, about 15–17 minutes. Cool several minutes before removing from the pans.

For the loaves, bake for 25–30 minutes until golden brown and loaves are baked through (a wooden skewer inserted should come out clean). Cool the brioche loaves briefly and unmold then onto a rack to cool completely.

Puff Pastry

This is a simplified version of classic puff pastry for use as a buttery crust for some of the egg pie or tart recipes.

MAKES ONE 10 X 14 X ¼-INCH SHEET

- 1 ⅔ cups all-purpose flour
- ½ tsp. salt
- 1 cup (2 sticks) cold unsalted butter, cut into ¼-inch dice

Place 1 ⅓ cups of the flour and the salt into the bowl of a food processor. Add ¼ cup of the butter pieces and pulse until just combined. In a medium mixing bowl, toss the remaining ⅓ cup flour with the remaining butter pieces until the butter is coated with flour. Add the remaining butter pieces to the food processor and pulse a few times to just combine. Add ⅓ cup cold water and pulse until the dough just sticks together.

Turn out the dough onto a lightly floured work surface and shape it into a ball. Roll the dough out to form a 10 x 14-inch rectangle. Fold the dough into thirds, creating a 3 x 14-inch rectangle. Fold into thirds again, this time creating a roughly 3 x 5-inch rectangle. Wrap the dough in plastic wrap and refrigerate for at least 1 hour until using. Dough may be refrigerated for up to 2 days or frozen for up to 1 month.

When ready to use, lightly flour a work surface and roll out the dough to the desired degree of thickness.

Rustic Sandwich Bread

Rustic Sandwich Bread

I call this "rustic" because it won't turn out looking like a loaf of commercial bread! In fact, it is even more beautiful. The bread has a very delicate crumb and is delicious as toast or part of a dish.

MAKES 1 LOAF

- ½ cup whole milk
- 5 tbsps. unsalted butter
- 3 cups all-purpose flour
- 2 tbsps. granulated sugar
- 1 tsp. salt
- 2 tsps. instant yeast

Heat the milk just to a boil in a small saucepan over medium high heat. Remove from the heat and stir in the butter until melted. Add ½ cup cold water to the milk. Combine the flour, sugar, salt and yeast in the bowl of a stand mixer (or in a large bowl if kneading by hand). Add the milk mixture and mix to combine. Switch to the dough hook (or turn the mixture onto a lightly floured surface) and knead for 8 minutes, until dough is elastic. Transfer the dough to a lightly greased bowl and turn over to coat the top. Cover the bowl and allow the dough to rise in a warm place until doubled, about 1 ½ 2 hours.

Lightly grease an 8 ½ x 4 ½-inch loaf pan. On a lightly floured surface, press the ball of dough into an 8 x 12-inch rectangle. Starting at a short end, fold it into thirds, as if folding a letter. Repeat again, tucking in the ends of the loaf. Place the dough seam side down into the pan and cover loosely with buttered plastic wrap. Allow the dough to rise in a warm place above the edge of the pan until it has doubled in size and will spring back slowly when poked with a finger, about 1-1 ½ hours.

Preheat the oven to 375 degrees F. Bake the bread for 30-35 minutes, until the top is golden brown. Turn the loaf out of the pan onto a wire rack to cool before slicing.

Scrapple

Scrapple is typically a combination of offal (another word for organ meat) that is leftover from butchering. It is usually cooked with seasonings and then blended with cornmeal and buckwheat flour. The finished scrapple is pressed into a loaf pan and then sliced off and fried. If you knew what was in scrapple, would you eat it? People often assume the worst (and sometimes they are correct) as to what scraps go into making a commercial batch of scrapple. The solution? Make your own. By using pork ribs and ground pork, you can ensure that your scrapple is as wholesome as you want it to be. Homemade scrapple also tastes really good, so it makes it easier to say no to store-bought mystery meat. Scrapple doesn't freeze very well, so this batch is small enough to consume in a 1–2 weeks, if it lasts that long.

 **MAKES 1 LOAF**

- 2 lbs. bone-in pork ribs
- 1 lb. ground pork
- 1 ½ cups yellow cornmeal
- ½ cup buckwheat flour
- 2 tsps. salt
- 2 tsps. freshly ground pepper
- 1 tsp. ground sage
- ½ tsp. ground nutmeg
- ½ tsp. ground cloves

Cover the ribs with water in a large saucepan or Dutch oven. Simmer gently for 1 ½–2 hours, until the meat is separating from the bones.

Strain the broth into a clean bowl. Measure the broth to 2 quarts (if you do not have enough, add chicken stock to make 2 quarts). Heat the broth in a large saucepan or Dutch oven over medium-high heat. Stir the ground meat into the broth and bring to a simmer. Cook for 20 minutes. In the meantime, remove the meat and fat from the ribs. Discard the bones and run the meat through a meat grinder or food processor until coarsely ground. Stir the rib meat into the broth with the ground pork.

In a separate bowl, sift together the cornmeal, buckwheat flour, salt, pepper, sage, nutmeg and cloves. Gradually add to the simmering meat mixture, stirring constantly to eliminate lumps. Cook for 30 minutes, stirring often to prevent sticking. Add extra hot water or chicken stock as necessary if the mixture becomes too dry. After 30 minutes, the scrapple should acquire a thick, mashed-potato-like consistency. Remove the mixture from the heat and allow to cool slightly.

Lightly grease a an 8 ½ x 4 ½-inch loaf pan and spoon in the mixture. Tap the pan lightly on the counter to settle the mixture evenly. Allow the mixture to cool, then cover with plastic wrap and refrigerate overnight.

When ready to prepare, turn the scrapple out of the pan onto a cutting board and cut into ¼-inch-thick slices. Heat 2 tbsps. butter or oil in a large skillet over medium-high heat. Dredge the scrapple lightly in all-purpose flour and shake off any excess. Add a few slices of scrapple and turn heat to medium. Cook for 3–4 minutes per side, until brown, crispy and cooked through.

Sausage

All of the recipes for sausage begin with 8 ounces of ground pork. Simply combine the pork with the seasonings and mix well before cooking.

Andouille Sausage

Andouille sausage is typically smoked, so if possible, add smoked flavor to this version using a stovetop smoker or smoking gun (available on Amazon or at specialty kitchen stores). Even without the added smoke, this seasoning blend featuring smoked paprika will work well in recipes that call for Andouille. The texture of Andouille is finely ground, so, if possible, ask your butcher to run it through the grinder a second time.

 **MAKES 8 OZ.**

- 8 oz. ground pork
- 1 ½ tsps. chili powder
- 3 tbsps. smoked paprika
- 1 tsp. freshly ground black pepper
- ½ tsp. cayenne pepper
- ½ tsp. ground cumin
- 1 tsp. crushed red pepper
- 1 tsp. salt
- 2 tsps. minced garlic
- 1 tsp. dried oregano
- 1 tsp. dried thyme

Chorizo

Chorizo may be of either Spanish or Mexican origin, but both types are flavored with smoked paprika. The Spanish version is typically cured (like salami), so this version is more akin to the Mexican style, as it needs to be cooked.

 **MAKES 8 OZ.**

- 8 oz. ground pork
- 2 tsps. smoked paprika
- 1 tsp. freshly ground black pepper
- ½ tsp. cayenne pepper
- ½ tsp. ground cumin
- 1 tsp. crushed red pepper
- 1 tsp. salt
- 2 tsps. chili powder
- 2 tsps. dried oregano
- ¼ tsp. ground cloves
- 1 tsp. ground cumin

Italian Sausage

Italian sausage is flavored with fennel or anise and is often sold in two versions: sweet and hot. This blend is somewhere in the middle.

 **MAKES 8 OZ.**

- 8 oz. ground pork
- 2 tsps. minced garlic
- 1 tsp. crushed fennel seeds
- 1 tsp. freshly ground black pepper
- ¼ tsp. cayenne pepper
- 1 tsp. crushed red pepper
- 1 tsp. salt
- ½ tsp. chopped dried sage
- 1 tbsp. chopped flat-leaf

Chef's Tip: Sausage may be refrigerated uncooked for up to 2 days or frozen for up to 2 months.

Pesto

MAKES ½ CUP

- 1 cup fresh herb leaves (basil, tarragon, mint, etc.)
- 1 tsp. salt
- 1 tsp. minced garlic
- 2 tbsps. pine nuts, toasted
- 2 tbsps. grated Parmesan
- 6 tbsps. extra-virgin olive oil

Use a mortar and pestle to combine the herb, salt, garlic and pine nuts into a paste (or combine in a food processor). Stir in the cheese. Drizzle in the olive oil a few teaspoons at a time to combine. Refrigerate or freeze until ready to use.

Tomato Salsa

Hand chopping the tomatoes will result in a coarser texture than using a food processor, which can easily over-process them if you're not careful.

 **MAKES 1 CUP**

- 6 plum tomatoes, skins and seeds removed and coarsely chopped (see Chef's Tip)
- ½ sweet onion, coarsely chopped
- 4 scallions, trimmed and chopped
- 1 jalapeno pepper, seeded and finely chopped
- 1 tsp. minced garlic
- 2 tbsps. extra-virgin olive oil
- 3 tbsp. lime juice
- 3 tbsps. chopped fresh herb, like basil or cilantro, according to taste
- Salt and freshly ground pepper to taste

In a large bowl, mix together the tomatoes, onion, scallions, jalapeno and garlic. Stir in the olive oil, lime juice and herb. Season with salt and freshly grated black pepper to taste. Refrigerate until ready to use.

Chef's Tip: To remove the skin of tomatoes, bring a medium saucepan filled with water to a boil. Fill a medium bowl with ice and water. Cut a very shallow X on the bottom of the tomato with a paring knife. Drop the tomato into the boiling water. Remove it with a slotted spoon when the skin begins to peel, about 30–60 seconds. Submerge the tomato into the bowl of ice water. Allow it to cool completely, about 5 minutes. (This will ensure that the tomato does not continue cooking.) Remove the tomato from the ice water and peel the skin off. To remove the seeds, simply quarter the peeled tomato and use a spoon to scoop them out.

Hollandaise Sauce

This version of hollandaise uses white wine to flavor the acidic base.

 **MAKES 1 CUP**

- 3 large egg yolks
- 1 tsp. lemon juice
- ¼ cup dry white wine
- 1 tsp. chopped shallots
- ½ cup unsalted clarified butter (see Chef's Tip)
- ½ tsp. salt

Whisk together the egg yolks and lemon juice and set aside. Place a stainless bowl over a saucepan containing barely simmering water (or use a double boiler). The water should not be touching the bottom of the bowl. Add the white wine and shallots and cook until liquid is reduced to 2 tablespoons. Strain out the shallots and return the liquid to the heat. Whisk in the egg yolk mixture. (If the eggs get too hot and start to break, remove the pan from the heat and whisk a few drops of cool water into the mixture.) Continue whisking until the mixture is thickened and doubled in volume. Remove the mixture from the heat. Add a few drops of the melted butter, whisking it in quickly to emulsify. Drizzle in the remaining butter, whisking continuously until it's all incorporated. Stir in the salt and serve warm.

Chef's Tip: To make the clarified butter, melt 12 ounces (1 ½ sticks) butter in a saucepan over low heat (or use the microwave) until the foam rises to the top of the melted butter. Skim the froth off the top and slowly pour the liquid into a measuring cup, discarding the milky solids in the bottom.

Crème Fraiche

Crème fraiche is widely available in groceries but it's equally as easy to make at home. It is stable when heated and adds a creamy accent to soups and other hot dishes. Making crème fraiche requires a little preplanning, since the ingredients must be assembled at least the night before.

 **MAKES 1 CUP**

- ½ cup sour cream
- ½ cup heavy cream

Whisk together the sour cream and heavy cream in a metal or glass bowl and cover loosely with plastic wrap. Allow the mixture to ripen at room temperature for at least 12 hours, until the mixture has thickened. Whisk the mixture, cover and refrigerate until using.

Bacon Jam

This bacon jam is included as part of the egg muffin recipe on p. 161 but is delicious served on toast with a wide array of egg dishes.

MAKES ABOUT 2 ½ CUPS

- 1 ½ pounds bacon, cut crosswise into 1-inch pieces, at room temperature
- 2 tsps. unsalted butter
- 1 large sweet onion, peeled and cut into ⅛-inch dice (about 1 ½ cups)
- 2 tsps. minced garlic
- ¼ cup apple cider vinegar
- ¼ cup muscovado sugar (or use dark brown)
- 3 tbsps. maple syrup
- 3 tbsps. bourbon (optional)
- ¼ tsp. ground allspice
- 1 tsp. chopped fresh thyme
- ½ tsp. finely ground black pepper
- 1 tbsp. extra-virgin olive oil

Line a large baking sheet with 2 layers of paper towels and set aside.

Add the bacon to a large skillet (or use a 5 to 6 qt. cast-iron Dutch oven) and heat over low. Cook the bacon, turning as needed, until the fat is rendered and the bacon is lightly browned all over, about 12–15 minutes. Use tongs to transfer the bacon to the baking sheet to drain. Allow to cool slightly. Finely chop bacon (or transfer the bacon to a food processor and process until crumbled). Set aside.

Pour off all but about 1 tbsp. of bacon fat from the pan. Discard the remaining fat or reserve for another use. Add the butter and heat until melted, about 1 minute. Add the onion to the pan and cook over medium heat, stirring often, until translucent, about 7–10 minutes. Add the garlic and cook for 30 seconds longer. Add ½ cup water, vinegar, muscovado sugar, maple syrup, bourbon (if using), allspice, thyme and black pepper, and bring to a boil. Lower to a simmer and cook, stirring and scraping up any browned bits, for 2 minutes. Add the bacon and stir to combine.

Cook uncovered, stirring often, until the liquid is almost completely evaporated and the mixture is brown and has a jam-like consistency, about 13–15 minutes.

Remove from the heat and stir in the olive oil. Allow the bacon mixture to cool slightly. Spoon the mixture into a sealable container and refrigerate for up to 4 weeks. Serve at room temperature or transfer to a pan and rewarm gently over low heat if desired prior to serving.

INDEX

Almond-Crusted Crab Cakes with Eggs, 187
Almonds
  Almond-Crusted Crab Cakes with Eggs, 187
Anchovy
  Mediterranean Eggs, 155
  Egg Pie with Roasted Garlic, Tomatoes and Eggplant, 168
Andouille
  Andouille Sausage, 218
  Andouille Sausage Strata, 141
Andouille Sausage Strata, 141
Arborio rice
  Mushroom Risotto with Eggs, 97
Asparagus
  Asparagus and Sweet Onion Tart, 105
  Eggs Lobster Oscar, 107
  Eggs with Pesto, Leeks and Asparagus, 99
  French omelet fillings, 65
  How To Blanch, 100
Asparagus and Sweet Onion Tart, 105

Avocado
  Bacon Jam, Avocado and Egg Muffin Sandwiches, 161
  Breakfast Quesadilla, 147
Bacon
  Bacon Jam, 225
  Bacon Jam, Avocado and Egg Muffin Sandwiches, 161
  Eggs Benedict, 51
  Eggs in Potato Nests with Canadian Bacon, 67
Bacon Jam, 225
Bacon Jam, Avocado and Egg Muffin Sandwiches, 161
Baked Eggs, 44
Baked Polenta with Eggs, Sausage and Fontina, 111
Baked Tomato, Egg and Mozzarella in Phyllo Cups, 87
Balsamic vinegar
  Portobello Mushrooms with Basil Egg Topping, 93
  Quinoa with Tomato, Basil, Mozzarella and Eggs, 83

Basil
  Eggs with Pesto, Leeks and Asparagus, 99
  Eggs with Roasted Cherry Tomatoes, 75
  Gorgonzola Sausage Frittata, 135
  Italian Frittata, 69
  Pesto, 221
  Prosciutto and Ricotta Cheese Pie, Portobello Mushrooms with Basil Egg Topping, 93
  Quinoa with Tomato, Basil, Mozzarella and Eggs, 83
  Rolled Basil Soufflé with Roasted Red Pepper Coulis, 153
Bean threads
  Spring Rolls with Eggs, Mushrooms and Sausage, 163
Beans
  Huevos Rancheros, 61
Beef
  Corned Beef Brisket Hash with Poached Eggs and Horseradish, 115

Steak and Eggs with Cheese Grits, 159
Steak, Eggs and Waffles with Chimichurri, 119
Blini
   Nested Eggs with Potato Blini and Dill Cream, 199
Bread crumbs
   Almond-Crusted Crab Cakes with Eggs, 187
   Andouille Sausage Strata, 141
   Cheese and Egg Souffle, 77
   Egg Custard with Morels, 106
   Macaroni and Cheese with Eggs, 79
Breakfast Burritos with Chicken, Eggs and Salsa, 143
Breakfast Quesadillas, 147
Brie
   Ham and Brie Soufflé, 155
   Oven Puffed Lobster and Brie Custards, 191
   Potato Skins with Egg, Tomato and Brie, 91
Brioche, 211
   Andouille Sausage Strata, 141
   Eggs and Mushrooms in Brioche, 103

Eggs with Brioche and Caramelized Onions, 108
Smoked Salmon and Eggs with Spinach, 173
Buckwheat flour
   Scrapple, 216
Canadian bacon
   Eggs Benedict, 51
Capers
   Egg Pie with Roasted Garlic, Tomatoes and Eggplant, 188
   Mediterranean Eggs, 175
Carnaroli rice
   Mushroom Risotto with Eggs, 97
Caviar
   Custard Eggs with Potatoes and Caviar, 179
   Nested Eggs with Potato Blini and Dill Cream, 199
Cheddar
   Andouille Sausage Strata, 141
   Breakfast Burritos with Chicken, Eggs and Salsa, 143
   Corn Pudding with Cilantro and Chorizo, 127
Cheese (*see specific type*)
   Cheese and Egg Soufflé, 77

Chevre (*see also goat cheese*)
   Eggs with Prosciutto, Sun-Dried Tomatoes and Chevre, 131
Chicken
   Breakfast Burritos with Chicken, Egg and Salsa, 143
Chiffonade, 75
Chili peppers
   Soft-Cooked Eggs with Chili-Infused Honey, 95
Chimichurri
   Steak, Egg and Waffles with Chimichurri, 119
Clarified butter
   Eggs Benedict, 51
   Hollandaise, 223
Coddled Eggs, 42
   Eggs with Prosciutto, Sun-Dried Tomatoes and Chevre, 131
Corn Pudding with Cilantro and Chorizo, 127
Corned beef brisket
   Corned Beef Brisket Hash with Poached Eggs and Horseradish, 115
   Corned Beef Brisket Hash with Poached Eggs and Horseradish, 115
Crab and Eggs in Chive Crepes, 183

Crepes
  Crab and Eggs in Chive Crepes, 183
  Eggs with Salmon in Dill Crepes, 169
Crabmeat
  Almond-Crusted Crab Cakes with Eggs, 187
  Crab and Eggs in Chive Crepes, 183
Crème Fraiche, 225
Croque Madame, 53
Custard Eggs in Potatoes with Caviar, 179
Dill
  Smoked Salmon and Goat Cheese Souffles, 167
  Eggs with Salmon in Dill Crepes, 169
Duck confit
  Duck Confit Hash with Mushrooms, 125
Duck Confit Hash with Mushrooms, 125
Egg Custard with Morels, 106
Egg Pie with Roasted Garlic, Tomatoes and Eggplant, 188
Eggplant
  Egg Pie with Roasted Garlic, Tomatoes and Eggplant, 188
  Mediterranean Eggs, 175
Eggs and Mushrooms in Brioche, 103

Eggs Benedict, 51
Eggs in a Basket, 59
Eggs in Potato Nests with Bacon, 67
Eggs Lobster Oscar with Tarragon Rounds, 107
Egg Pie with Roasted Garlic, Tomatoes and Eggplant, 168
Eggs Poached in Tomato Sauce, 57
Eggs with Brioche and Caramelized Onions, 108
Eggs with Kale and Pancetta, 139
Eggs with Pesto, Leeks and Asparagus, 99
Eggs with Prosciutto, Sun-Dried Tomatoes and Chevre, 131
Eggs with Roasted Cherry Tomatoes, 75
Eggs with Salmon in Dill Crepes, 169
English Muffins, 205
Feta
  Eggs Poached in Tomato Sauce, 57
Fish sauce
  Thai Fried Rice with Eggs, Pork Belly and Frizzled Leeks, 117
Flour Tortillas, 207
Fontina
  Baked Polenta with Eggs, Sausage and Fontina, 111
  Cheese and Egg Soufflé, 77

French Omelet, 63
Fried Eggs, 45
Frittata
  Gorgonzola Sausage Frittata, 135
  Italian Frittata, 69
  Smoked Trout Frittata with Potatoes, Horseradish and Chives,
Ginger
  Thai Fried Rice with Eggs, Pork Belly and Frizzled Leeks, 117
Goat cheese (see also chevre)
  Asparagus and Sweet Onion Tart, 105
  Breakfast Quesadilla, 147
  Cheese and Egg Souffle, 77
  Portobello Mushrooms with Basil Egg Topping, 93
  Rolled Basil Souffle with Roasted Red Pepper Coulis, 153
  Smoked Salmon and Goat Cheese Souffles, 167
Gorgonzola
  Gorgonzola Sausage Frittata, 135
Lentils with Prosciutto and Eggs, 149

Wilted Spinach and Gorgonzola Omelet Roll, 85
Gorgonzola Sausage Frittata, 135
Grits
   Steak and Egg with Cheese Grits, 159
Gruyère
   Croque Madame, 53
   Lobster and Thyme Quiche, 193
   Macaroni and Cheese with Eggs, 79
Ham
   Ham and Brie Souffle Roll, 155
Ham and Brie Souffle Roll, 155
Hard-Cooked Eggs, 37
Egg Pie with Roasted Garlic, Tomatoes and Eggplant, 188
Hoagie Rolls, 208
   Scrapple and Egg Hoagie, 163
Hoagie Rolls, 208
Hollandaise Sauce, 223
Honey
   Soft-Cooked Eggs with Chili-Infused Honey, 95
Horseradish
   Corned Beef Brisket Hash with Poached Eggs and Horseradish, 115
   Smoked Trout Frittata with Potatoes, Horseradish and Chives, 185

Huevos Rancheros, 61
Italian Frittata, 69
Jalapeno
   Breakfast Burritos with Chicken, Eggs and Salsa, 143
   Breakfast Quesadilla, 147
   Corn Pudding with Cilantro and Chorizo, 127
   Huevos Rancheros, 61
   Tomato Salsa, 222
Jam, bacon, 225
Leeks
   Eggs with Pesto, Leeks and Asparagus, 99
   Thai Fried Rice with Eggs, Pork Belly and Frizzled Leeks, 117
Lentils
   Lentils with Prosciutto and Eggs, 149
Lentils with Prosciutto and Eggs, 149
Lobster
   Eggs Lobster Oscar with Tarragon Rounds, 107
   Oven-Puffed Lobster and Brie Custards, 191
   Lobster and Thyme Quiche, 193
Lobster and Thyme Quiche, 193
Macaroni and Cheese with Eggs, 79

Mascarpone
   Salami and Egg Tarts in Polenta Crust, 133
Mediterranean Eggs, 175
Mint
   Eggs Poached in Tomato Sauce, 57
   Spring Rolls with Eggs, Mushrooms and Sausage, 163
Morels
   Egg Custard with Morels, 106
Mozzarella
   Baked Tomato, Egg and Mozzarella in Phyllo Cups, 87
   Quinoa with Tomato, Basil, Mozzarella and Eggs, 83
   Mushroom Risotto with Eggs, 97
Mushrooms
   Mushroom Risotto with Eggs, 97
Nested Eggs with Potato Blini and Dill Cream, 199
Oven-Puffed Lobster and Brie Custards, 191
Parmesan
   Baked Polenta with Eggs, Sausage and Fontina, 111
   Cheese and Egg Souffle, 77
   Croque Madame, 53
   Italian Frittata, 69
   Mushroom Risotto with Eggs, 97

Pesto, 221
Prosciutto and
   Ricotta Cheese Egg
   Pie, 157
Pecorino
   Cheese and Egg
   Soufflé, 77
Pesto, 221
Phyllo, 87
Pine nuts
   Pesto, 221
Poached Eggs, 38
Polenta
   Baked Polenta with
      Eggs, Sausage and
      Fontina, 111
   Salami and Egg
      Tarts in Polenta
      Crust, 133
Porcini
   Duck Confit Hash
      with Eggs and
      Mushrooms, 125
   Mushroom Risotto
      with Eggs, 97
Pork
   Thai Fried Rice with
      Eggs, Pork Belly
      and Frizzled
      Leeks, 117
   Sausage, 218
   Scrapple, 216
   Spring Rolls with
      Eggs, Mushrooms
      and Sausage, 163
Pork belly
   Thai Fried Rice with
      Eggs, Pork Belly and
      Frizzled Leeks, 117

Portobello Mushrooms
   with Basil Egg
   Topping, 93
Potato Skins with Egg,
   Tomato and Brie, 91
Prosciutto
   Eggs with Prosciutto,
      Sun-Dried
      Tomatoes and
      Chevre, 131
   Lentils with
      Prosciutto and
      Eggs, 149
   Prosciutto and
      Ricotta Cheese
      Pie, 157
   Rolled Basil Souffle
      with Roasted Red
      Pepper Coulis, 153
Prosciutto and Ricotta
   Cheese Pie, 157
Provolone
   Scrapple and Egg
      Hoagie, 163
Puff Pastry, 213
   Asparagus and Sweet
      Onion Tart, 105
   Egg Pie with Roasted
      Garlic, Tomatoes
      and Eggplant, 188
Queso fresco
   Huevos Rancheros, 61
Quiche
   Lobster and Thyme
      Quiche, 193
Quinoa
   Quinoa with Tomato,
      Basil, Mozzarella
      and Eggs, 83

Quinoa with Tomato,
   Basil, Mozzarella and
   Eggs, 83
Red pepper
   Andouille Sausage
      Strata, 141
   Rolled Basil Souffle
      with Roasted Red
      Pepper Coulis, 153
Rice
   Mushroom Risotto
      with Eggs, 97
   Thai Fried Rice with
      Eggs, Pork Belly and
      Frizzled Leeks, 117
Rice paper rounds
   Spring Rolls with
      Eggs, Mushrooms
      and Sausage, 163
Ricotta
   Prosciutto and
      Ricotta Cheese
      Pie, 157
   Salami and Egg Tarts
      in Polenta Crust, 133
   Rolled Basil Souffle with
      Roasted Red Pepper
      Coulis, 153
Rustic Sandwich
   Bread, 215
   Eggs in a Basket, 53
Salami
   Salami and Egg
      Tarts in Polenta
      Crust, 133
Salami and Egg Tarts in
   Polenta Crust, 133
Sausage, 218
   Andouille Sausage
      Strata, 141

INDEX   231

Baked Polenta with Eggs, Sausage and Fontina, 111
Gorgonzola Sausage Frittata, 135
Huevos Rancheros, 61
Spring Rolls with Eggs, Mushrooms and Sausage, 163
Scrambled Eggs, 40
Scrapple, 216
  Scrapple and Egg Hoagie, 163
Scrapple and Egg Hoagie, 163
Smoked salmon
  Eggs with Salmon in Dill Crepes, 169
  Smoked Salmon and Eggs with Spinach, 173
Smoked Salmon and Eggs with Spinach, 173
Smoked Salmon and Goat Cheese Souffles, 167
Smoked trout
  Smoked Trout Frittata with Potatoes, Horseradish and Chives, 185
Smoked Trout Frittata with Potatoes, Horseradish and Chives, 185
Soft-Cooked Eggs
  Soft-Cooked Eggs with Chili-Infused Honey, 95
Soft-Cooked Eggs with Chili-Infused Honey, 95
Soufflé
  Cheese and Egg Soufflé, 77
  Ham and Brie Soufflé Roll, 155
  Rolled Basil Soufflé with Roasted Red Pepper Coulis, 153
  Smoked Salmon and Goat Cheese Souffles, 167
Spanish Tortilla, 71
Spinach
  Smoked Salmon and Eggs with Spinach, 173
  Wilted Spinach and Gorgonzola Omelet Roll, 85
Spring Rolls with Eggs, Mushrooms and Sausage, 163
Steak and Egg with Cheese Grits, 159
Steak, Egg and Waffles with Chimichurri, 119
Tarragon rounds
  Eggs Lobster Oscar with Tarragon Rounds, 107
Thai Fried Rice with Eggs, Pork Belly and Frizzled Leeks, 117
Thyme
  Lobster and Thyme Quiche, 193
Tomato Salsa, 222
  Breakfast Burritos with Chicken, Eggs and Salsa, 143
Truffle, black
Wilted Spinach and Gorgonzola Omelet Roll, 85
Yeast
  Brioche, 211
  English Muffins, 205
  Hoagie Rolls, 208
  Rustic Sandwich Bread, 215
Zucchini
  Italian frittata, 69

Photo on p. 107 : Betty Swora/Shutterstock
Thank you!

Thank you for purchasing this book. I am pleased to have you along for the journey to better health and better eating. I know you could have picked from dozens of cookbooks, so to show my appreciation I'd like to offer you a bonus: *Eggs for Breakfast: Ten Quick and Delicious Recipes for Weekdays*. Simply sign up on my website www.donnaleahy.com and I will send you the PDF. I will include you on my list for free stuff and also periodically send you exclusive special offerings as well.

As an experienced chef and author, I write cookbooks on a variety of topics and themes, so my other cookbooks may interest you as well. Please feel free to let me know what aspects of the book you enjoyed and what things you wish I had included. If you have any suggestions for future topics, I'd love to hear them as well.

Finally, if you have a moment to [review this book on Amazon](), I'd really appreciate it. This type of feedback will help me continue to write the kind of cookbooks that you want to use. Thanks again, I look forward to hearing from you.

Chef Donna

www.ingramcontent.com/pod-product-compliance
Lightning Source LLC
Chambersburg PA
CBHW052022070526
44584CB00016B/1862